LEADING

The Art of Becoming
an Executive

Other McGraw-Hill Titles by Philip B. Crosby

Quality Is Free: The Art of Making Quality Certain   (1979)

Quality Without Tears: The Art of Hassle-Free Management   (1984)

Running Things: The Art of Making Things Happen   (1986)

The Eternally Successful Organization: The Art of Corporate Wellness   (1988)

Let's Talk Quality: 96 Questions You Always Wanted to Ask Phil Crosby   (1989)

LEADING

The Art of Becoming an Executive

Philip B. Crosby

McGraw-Hill Publishing Company

New York St. Louis San Francisco Auckland
Bogotá Caracas Hamburg Lisbon London Madrid
Mexico Milan Montreal New Delhi Oklahoma City
Paris San Juan São Paulo Singapore
Sydney Tokyo Toronto

Dedicated to
Victoria Antoinette Crosby,
age five going on twenty-one

Library of Congress Cataloging-in-Publication Data

Crosby, Philip B.
  Leading, the art of becoming an executive / Philip B. Crosby.
    p. cm.
  ISBN 0-07-014567-9
  1. Leadership. 2. Executive ability. I. Title.
HD57.7.C755 1990   89-36427
658.4'092—dc20   CIP

34567890 DOC/DOC 95432109

ISBN 0-07-014567-9

*The editors for this book were Jim Bessent and Barbara B. Toniolo,
the designer was Naomi Auerbach, and the production supervisor
was Suzanne W. Babeuf. It was composed by the McGraw-Hill
Publishing Company Professional & Reference Division
Composition Unit.*

Printed and bound by R. R. Donnelley & Sons Company.

A sixty-minute audio program to accompany this book
is now available. Ask for it at your local bookstore
or phone toll-free 1-800-2-MCGRAW.

*For more information about other McGraw-Hill materials,
call 1-800-2-MCGRAW in the United States. In other
countries, call your nearest McGraw-Hill Office.*

Contents

Preface   vii

Introduction   1

Part 1. The Three Principles of Leading

   1. Executive Focus   7
   2. Relationships   27
   3. Quality   39
   4. Finance   53

Part 2. Five Variations on the Theme of Becoming a Leader

   5. A New Beginning   69
   6. Organizing Kargston Associates   81
   7. The Participants   93
   8. Class Introduction: "A Day at the Movies"   101
   9. Elizabeth   123

10. Nick   137
11. Anna   153
12. Harold   171
13. Alvin   185
14. Graduation Celebration   199
15. Guidelines for Browsers   203

Index   212

Preface

I deliberately set out on the road from manager to executive in order to improve my life and contribution. This book is meant to contain some of the useful things I have learned on that path. It is not biographical at all since most of what I learned came from watching others try to climb mountains in evening dress. But there are some basics, and once a person understands the concepts of being an executive and develops the proper attitude, there is no difficulty in finding that kind of work. The world is overflowing with managers. There is a critical shortage of executives.

One of the most important things an executive needs to learn is that a good manager can run about anything, but a good executive is limited to things that can be understood. The navigator needs to know all about steering, but the captain must understand the mission, the direction, the political ramifications, and the effect that turning the ship will have on the banquet being served below. Very few conglomerates have been successful for this reason. The captain must really understand the world of shipping. The managers can handle most of what comes up.

For instance, I know as much about running things as anyone can expect to accumulate in 40 years of effort. Financial systems, human resources, people motivation, inventory control, quality, all of those things and more are within my experience. My career started at the bottom and touched every rung on the way up. I sat at Harold Geneen's table for 14 years and participated in about every event known to the world of management. I founded a company and served as its CEO for 9 years during which it grew into a solid and debt-free worldwide concern. I've been through about everything that can happen from being way up to scrambling desperately for survival.

However, if you ask me, "What color are women going to want next year?" or "How should we design the rooms in our new hotel?" or "What price should we put on this or that new product?" or a hundred other questions about a specific item, I will probably not know the answer. Nobody knows everything about everything.

I knew the quality business and I knew consulting. Therefore I could deal with specific questions in starting PCA. However, if we had followed some of the advice offered, we could have purchased a hotel or restaurant. Had we done so, it would have been a mistake for me to start setting menus or laying out rooms. I can cause it to happen and determine if I like the result, but I just do not know enough about the nuts and bolts of those businesses to make them successful.

That is where many who would have been conglomerates went up on the shoals. Instead of finding people who really understood each business, giving them clear requirements, and then letting them run their operations (like Harold Geneen did), most tried to do it all. In an era where athletic teams have specialists for everything, it should be apparent that the powerful "know everything" executive is obsolete, if indeed such a person ever really did exist.

The overall running of the organization and the selection of work for managers to do is what executives are all about. They have to create an environment that will encourage great work; they have to establish a broad vision of the organization and its purpose that everyone can understand; they have to keep up with the present and yet know what is around the bend; they have to continually make certain that people know what they are doing.

This last part is harder than it seems. I have met very few people who really knew what they were doing and even fewer who recognized that. We are a lot better off when we know our limits and proceed to operate by obtaining counsel where it is required. Then we can do what our judgment tells us, but on an informed basis. Those who just plow ahead on instinct will not be right enough times.

Since there is no absolute right or wrong in the executive world, this book has been structured in a "conversational learning format." In trying to put together something that would be more interesting than just another management tome, I thought about the "Young Dr. Kildare" series of films, which was very big during my formative years. Lew Ayres was the young man and Lionel Barrymore played Dr. Gillespie, the irascible old diagnostician with a heart of gold who taught young physicians about life and the business of healing. Everyone seemed to enjoy themselves while learning from his experiences. That format seemed to provide a way of bringing out pertinent issues.

I cannot write in "irascible" style, but I did try to make the conversations realistic while making the points clear. There is no reason people should have to have their heads blown off before realizing that the gun is loaded.

I am trying to become a full-time writer and speaker instead of being an executive. Peggy and I built a new home in Winter Park and included a library for that purpose. A lot of this book was written while all that was going on. At the same time, PCA is continuing its expansion and we are required to travel around to talk with clients and other folks. Thus a great deal has been written on a portable computer/word processor in various hotel rooms and on various airplanes.

This reinforces for me that we live in a world economy and

a world business environment. Except for cultural and social graces, I find little difference in the opportunities and problems presented to executives everywhere. If governments could ever come together as well as business leaders do, most of the hassle would go out of the world.

I would like to thank my wife Peggy for her support in all this. She insists that I work hard at keeping well in order to be able to do everything else. That is really good advice from a really good executive.

PHIL CROSBY
Winter Park, Florida

Introduction

The Executive Profile

Executives determine what is going to be run; managers do the running.

Learning to become a manager is a worthwhile effort that provides a great deal of personal satisfaction. Without managers there could be no world worth living in. Without managers very little would happen.

But without executives the managers would have nothing to manage. The executive thinks up the venture; the executive determines what has to be done; the executive delegates the jobs necessary to achieve the desired result. The executive establishes the requirements. The executive also makes most of the money and leads the league in opportunity to accumulate wealth.

But having a sign on the office door or carrying a well-embossed business card does not make one an executive. One *is* if one *does*. One *is not* if one *does not*. Yet it is possible to learn how to become an executive. Most of it is conceptual; a lot is energy; the majority is direction.

Executives must always keep their eyes on the real objective, while being up-to-date on what is really going on "out there." It is like taking a boat up the Amazon, working on a convincing welcoming speech to the headhunters, and at the same time assuring that someone is making certain that the river-depth machine is performing.

The producer of a motion picture is an executive. He or she has the responsibilities of finding the script, digging up the money, determining the talent, laying out the promotion and distribution plan, keeping the director within budget, soothing the stars' feelings, causing theaters to be clean, and keeping peace on the sets—all while appearing confident that everything is going to work out.

The executive sees the need for each of these components of the project, and assigns them to someone to manage—under direction. Every task is original even though many are a traditional part of the business. Managers learn how to set up budgets, obtain proper approvals, and measure the progress of work. The way the executive sets up and directs the managers of the project predetermines the degree of success. All components have to work, both individually and in concert, for the whole scheme to be accomplished.

A wonderful script can be ruined by inappropriate actors. Adequate financing can be drowned by cost overruns. A negative advertising campaign can produce empty seats. Poor relationships can poison the entire project. The opportunities for problems are limitless, yet there are few new ways to fail.

Someone has to keep all of this in hand. Someone has to be aware of sounds and silences. Someone has to know when it is time to do something that no one else is aware of. That person is the executive. Well-informed, confident, possessed of interpersonal skills, not a superperson, usually not even exceptionally gifted—the executive hears all, sees all, and feels all.

Leadership Can Be Learned

One can learn to be an executive: in fact, that is the way executives are made. I was a manager for several years and assumed that I was an executive. I had a budget, a staff, a work force, meetings, problems, and a full schedule. What else was necessary? There were several hundred persons in my department, and people were yelling at us all the time, so I must have been an executive.

One day as we sat around waiting for the boss's staff meeting to begin, someone said, "What is the difference between a program manager and a program director?" Before anyone could answer, the personnel director said, "About $15,000 a year."

We all laughed and the world went on, but the comparison stuck in my mind. My total compensation at that time was about $20,000 a year as a program manager. I worked for a project director, and he worked for the general manager. The general manager worked for corporate headquarters, and they had lots of people up there who never got yelled at. It was beginning to occur to me that my view of the business world was somewhat limited. I needed to know more, and I needed to get to an organizational level where there was a lot more latitude of movement and a lot more opportunity to be properly rewarded for my efforts.

I already knew that those who did the hardest work did not necessarily make the most money. (Watching my lawyer earn five hundred dollars for a couple of hours work taught me that.) I also knew that demonstrating the ability to get the impossible done in a manager's job just meant that even more impossible tasks would soon be coming my way. Those in the higher organizational levels usually did not recognize a great accomplishment when they saw it. Most of their measurements were ineffectual, which meant that the effective and the sloppy looked much the same to them. They went on personality more than anything else when it came to evaluating people.

A Most Useful Vow

My first vow as an "executive-to-be" was that I would not forget what it was like to be on the lower levels. ("I used to be an enlisted man myself, son.") That turned out to be a useful vow. People relate to someone they recognize as having an understanding of life in the working lane, and who they feel has empathy for the pressures and frustrations that exist there. They help make those executives successful, just as they help make those who do not relate to them unsuccessful. Most executives would not recognize that their subordinates might be deliberately working against them. Senior executives are sometimes baffled by the successful pattern of some leaders and the failure rate of others. It never dawns on them that the pieces on the chessboard are fixing the game in favor of those who appreciate them. I saw a lot of this during my military career in two wars. All my time was spent in the enlisted ranks. We had our own rules, and we responded to those officers who responded to us. We made some of them very successful, and we let others fall to their natural level. Some of our leaders pretended to relate and some actually did. We could always tell the difference. It is not possible to fool the people for very long. Once in a while they are wrong in judging those who are given authority over them, but they catch on very quickly.

PART 1

The Three Principles of Leading

1
Executive Focus

Self-Administering the "Executives' Oath"

Something that sticks in my mind after all these years is what I learned as a member of the Boy Scouts. With a little effort I can still recall the Scout Oath and the list of characteristics that a Scout should strive to possess. These were very useful to me as a young boy because they represented a clear statement about what we should aspire to be. Corny? Perhaps. But it was the first documented, repeatable, and clear statement of personal policy I had run into. (The adults in any child's life usually think they explain policy to the child, but most of that is on the "close your mouth when you eat" level.)

In thinking about leadership I came to the conclusion that leaders could use a similar list of desirable aspirations. If we are going to learn to be executives, we might well examine what could be called the "characteristics of leadership." Leaders are:

- Willing to learn
- Ethical
- Available

- Determined
- Energetic
- Reliable
- Sensible
- Humble
- Intense
- Pleasant

To take a broader view of the content, consider each characteristic of leadership in detail.

An Executive Is a Learner

If anything is certain, it is that change is certain. The world we are making plans about today will not exist in this form tomorrow. The constant flow of information and the altering of ideas require that the executive keep learning. No one ever comes close to knowing it all. The business desert is layered with the bones of those who felt they understood completely and stopped learning. The entire problem of quality, for instance, could have been prevented if executives had open minds on the subject. Even today, when companies are working hard on quality, many executives feel they have learned all that is necessary. Yet no organization that I know of routinely produces defect-free products and services. Several are close, and they are continuing to work very hard. Such production is not difficult to accomplish: the information required exists, and there is a great deal of proof to be seen. However, it is hard to interest people in learning things they think they already know.

Almost every business distress comes about because of this unwillingness to learn or recognize reality. A few years back, the large-computer manufacturers dismissed the personal computer as a Christmas toy in much the same way that large-automobile makers viewed the small car. Likewise, financial executives were so anxious to lend money, they would not pay attention to those who showed that third world nations could not begin to repay them. For that matter, in almost every business failure the situation as it developed was known and could have been prevented, just like most political disasters. The executive has to reach out continually for information. Making a wrong decision is understandable; refusing to search continually for learning is not.

An Executive Is Ethical

The best reputation a leader can possess relates to displaying ethical conduct in all things. Those who are known for demonstrating such behavior are trusted and respected. They are never asked to do anything shady; they get to do what they want to do. Those who cry for a list of what is and what is not ethical are going to always have problems along this line. Unethical conduct is known by those who consider it. This is something that requires a clear policy and clear action if the policy is broken.

An Executive Is Available

People who are influenced or controlled by an executive need to feel that they can have personal access, if necessary. Face-to-face discussions are not always possible in huge organizations, but access in written form is a viable option. Confidential letters or memos should be able to get through even a tangled bureaucracy. In smaller operations the executive needs to get about and must also be willing to talk to anyone who shows up.

People want their leaders to be real people. They want to know that there is not a surrounding layer of underlings who prevent coworkers from reaching the executive with important information. They want to know that the executive, who is supposed to be the smartest of the bunch, will have the opportunity to pass judgment on what is happening in the company. If employees do not gain this feeling, they will be afraid to point out problems and situations. No one will ever know, for example, that the boiler has a tiny leak and that the crew leader does not plan to do anything about it.

An Executive Is Determined

The difference between a winning athlete and one who regularly comes close is not skill, it is the will to win—determination. Subordinates establish their personal determination level based on what they see in their leader. Wimpy behavior produces wimpy results.

An Executive Is Energetic

Serious people exude obvious energy. It may not be physically obvious, such as in bustling about, but it is apparent. This provides a confidence-building source for others. Enthusiasm is the result of an energetic person's working on something that he or she finds keenly interesting. This means a leader should not accept any project that does not produce a tingle deep down. The people the executive leads will directly reflect the energy level they see and feel.

An Executive Is Reliable

Performance over time is the key to reliability. Does the leader forget promises, flip from fad to fad, change directions in midstream? While not being all that personally predictable, does the executive follow a pattern that lets people know what to expect? Nothing makes an organization ineffective as quickly as having to wonder what is going to please or displease the boss. It changes everyone's concentration. They do not have time to work on the business at hand if they have to wonder how the boss is feeling. The boss involved in substance abuse—like alcohol, cocaine, or food for that matter—has a personality that varies from moment to moment. I used to work with a boss who could not safely be approached after lunch. Reliability is a primary sign of the grown-up executive.

An Executive Is Sensible

In Woody Allen's movie *Bananas* the newly elected president of a Latin America republic makes a speech to announce that from now on, all underwear will be worn on the outside and that the national language will be Swedish. This is so far out of line with what is reasonable that everyone could agree that this was not a sensible president. Some who become executives feel that the power thus given to them grants permission to quit dealing with reality. While these executives may not demand that we wear our undergarments on the outside, they do more subtle things that, while appearing to be businesslike, can erode the operation.

Deciding to expand an operation to six minor cities while taking on a large investment in facilities and new people at headquarters could be an example. Constructing a shopping center or an 80-story skyscraper just because the money is available is where most of our "see-through" buildings come from. Accumulating debt to buy something that adds no value to the company; taking on a task that no one has ever been able to accomplish, and using the same failed technology; or hoping for government protection when clearly it is not politically possible are a few other current examples.

An Executive Is Humble

Since most of the egotists in the world seem to find their way into business, the truly humble have a hard time being recognized. It is very easy for executives to come to the conclusion that they are the beginning and end of everything that is happening. They can develop the attitude that they are the ones who have to think of everything and that they are not properly appreciated. As a result, they start to dominate every meeting and every relationship. This silences people and produces more of the "I'm-the-only-one-around-here-who-makes-the-place-go" attitude.

People who want to give the impression of being humble, yet do not want others to miss knowing something significant about them, use what I call "humilities." These are carefully crafted sentences which on the surface show the speaker to be a nonachiever or victim but convey a deeper message of superiority. A few humilities might be:

- "I never score well at Augusta; it seems to intimidate me."
- "*The Wall Street Journal* quoted me incorrectly one time, so I do not accept their calls any more."
- "I hate running 20 miles every morning."
- "Women are much more forward today."
- "Managing a lot of money is a real pain."

An Executive Is Intense

"Concentrated on the task" is another way of saying *intense,* and I mean it in the best possible sense. Mothers are intense when caring for their babies. They know that little Harry is unable to exist without complete care. As Harry grows, the intensity remains but actions change. The executive is concentrated, but other interests can grow and flourish. Intensity needs to be something that can be turned on like a spotlight.

A competent ship captain is a good example of properly managed and directed intensity: he or she makes certain that the crew is eating well while planning a letter home and ensuring the proper functioning of the ship—all at the same time.

An Executive Is Pleasant

The most powerful people I have met always have time for courtesy and personal concern. They know that they do not have to beat up on everyone to have it known that they are important. They greet people; they ask about families; they listen. Waiters like them—and not necessarily because they are good tippers. They are welcome everywhere.

Getting Inside the Executive Mind

Military combat—like skiing—has at least one predictable characteristic: while it is happening, there is no time to think about anything else. All other concerns disappear when an enemy bent on your destruction is creeping through the bushes toward your general area, or when random patches of ice appear behind equally random moguls. The mind concentrates so hard, the body grows weary. (That is why troops who may not actually have been touched by hostile fire are genuinely bedraggled when making their way out of the battle zone. The mind wears out the body.) No one can stay very long in that kind of situation. Given such circumstances, leadership may be easier to accept because those being led have a vital interest in the decisions and actions of the leader. They pay very close attention during meetings regardless of how informal the sessions might be. They thirst for information.

Questions such as "Where are we?" "What was that?" "Where are we going?" "Who is doing what?" become part of a continual discussion. The leader able to provide answers and direction gains complete obedience. People will hang on every word when they realize that their fate is involved. Situations do not have to be life or death for persons to pay attention. The thought of being without a job or funds or future can generate such a response.

Even with a dedicated following, however, leaders have still managed to lose battles, wars, and even nations because they concentrated on the wrong things. Few battles are lost because of a lack of courage or dedication on the part of the troops. The leadership has to set out almost deliberately to overcome the positive characteristics of its personnel if the operation is to fail.

Organizations of all sizes and purposes succeed or fail as the direct result of what the leadership does. If people are sent into the fray without the proper training or equipment, if they are given conflicting direction or none at all, if their questions are improperly answered, if the resources to support their efforts are not supplied, if the strategy of the enterprise is faulty—then all is lost.

The executives of the organization, who typically constitute much less than 1 percent of the corporate population, are the ones who are supposed to attend to all this. They are the ones with the largest compensation and the most information. They are the ones to get us where we are going.

Four Useful Lessons from the Past

Napoleon was a successful battlefield leader because he took very good care of his troops and because he learned how to keep track of what was happening. He was the first "information junkie" executive. He created an elite corps of couriers who rode between his headquarters and the field. They carried messages but also were trained as observers. This was a time when huge armies could pass within a few miles of each other and not notice. Napoleon's field commanders received daily orders from him concerning battle plans. At the same time, the ministers back in Paris were reading his plans for the future and taking appropriate action.

Churchill, a lukewarm peacetime executive, came into greatness under wartime conditions. When the game was survival, others accepted his ideas and direction. He was one of the few who actually affected the course of history by his knowledge and determination.

Eisenhower was effective in both war and peace because he concentrated on leadership through putting together a team with common goals and proper resources. He was a strong personality who built strong relationships and could handle difficult people.

Roosevelt was a marvelous people picker. He was able to find just the right person for the job and then provide inspirational leadership.

Those who run companies are there because they created the organization or are professional executives hired to manage the operation. They have to work in a world where people's lives include more than the business of the corporation. The employees are not under combat conditions, so now and then they think about things other than the company. They can daydream for a moment or two without the threat of exposing themselves to enemy fire. The leader has to learn how to keep everyone focusing on the tasks and goals that will make the corporation successful.

Eschewing the Narrow View: Proaction versus Reaction

For this purpose executives need to concentrate their thinking and energy on the three areas that support the entire operation: finance, quality, and relationships. Everything necessary for personal and corporate success lies within these three equal areas. They provide the foundation that carries and controls the organization. What must happen on a daily basis should originate in compliance with clear policies established by the executive. What happens long range needs to come from the same source and be consistent with this foundation. A French premier said that war was too important to be left up to the generals. Running a corporation is too important to be left up to the functional departments.

The days are gone when functional specialists can cope with the management of a company all by themselves. Their views are necessarily narrow and restricted and do not always

coincide with the brutal reality of our present world economy
and its requirements and relationships. When one deals continually and professionally with the matters of marketing,
quality, purchasing, finance, engineering, or such, it is possible to begin to think that this one area of specialty covers the
whole organization.

Executives who have become used to managing by answer-
ing the questions of specialists are finding themselves in deep
trouble. There is no place for this easy way of operating because it means that the agenda of the company will be based
on reacting to vertical thinking rather than guiding the enterprise on the basis of preestablished, broad-based policies.
Policies must cover all the bases and relate to all operations.
They have to incorporate thinking that is worldwide,
industrywide, and peoplewide.

It's the Same, Large or Small.   The size of the company
makes little difference as far as the need for specific policies
is concerned. The situations are the same. Fortune 500 companies have three more zeros on everything than their
smaller competitors, but outside of that there is little difference in the executive's role. International finance, for instance, applies the same rules to those who do only a few
hundred thousand dollars worth of overseas business as they
do to those who move billions of dollars. They must complete
the same forms, deal with currency translation, and have employees or agents who work under regulations that are not
easily understood.

The only companies able to survive and prosper in this difficult and challenging environment are those whose executives spend all their time dealing with the way the company
must be run rather than limiting themselves to reacting to
whatever comes up.

Making Time to Sit and Think.   When I was working my
way through the remote realms of corporate life, it was easy
to identify the executives. They wore harried expressions,

were always in a hurry, had briefcases and desks full of papers, and were obsessed with problem identification and solutions. They often expressed the wish that they could somehow be granted the time to "sit and think" about things. But, alas, it could never come about. They were continually at least one meeting behind and had to do their mail while flying off to look at a problem.

The companies ran themselves much like many parliamentary governments have done over the years. Elected and appointed officials changed rapidly as governments gained or lost confidence, but the civil service stayed the same. These permanent managers ran the country in accordance with customs and regulations already established. The fact that their ministers changed regularly did not affect work life. This all keeps everything moving, given a normal situation. But we hardly live in what could be classified as a normal or predictable situation.

The High Cost of Reactive Leadership: A Case in Point

When the United States began to feel competition from Japan, Germany, and other foreign nations in the late 1960s and early 1970s, a distinct culture shock was initiated. The first area to be affected was mass production. Television sets, steel, automobiles, textiles, components, and such began to feel strong, competitive pressure. Prices of the foreign goods were lower than U.S. produced material, and the products themselves were more reliable.

Defect rates in products and materials were significantly lower in the imported products. American producers screamed that the competition worked only because of price dumping and that the customers were ungrateful. They pressed vigorously for government actions. The customers, amazed that they could buy a television set that did not have to be fixed regularly or a car that did not spend its first six months at the dealer, leaped to embrace the new products.

Executives called in their functional specialists to find out what was at the core of this problem. These experts determined that there were many different causes; most came down to the fact that foreign companies and the customers were not playing fair.

TEXTILES: They do not comply with the accepted defect rates. Their product has fewer defects or none, so they must be spending a lot more money on quality. That means they are price dumping. Also, they do not have full lines. They are picking out niches in the market.

STEEL: Their labor rates are much less than ours, and their governments subsidize them. The steel they are shipping is better quality and more consistent than ours. But when their real costs are exposed, they will be found wanting.

AUTOMOBILES: Their labor rates are much lower, and they do not have any unions. The cars they make are much less complicated than ours, without all the options. The Volkswagen does not even have a gas gauge. Their workers are better disciplined and more cooperative than ours. We need protection.

TELEVISION SETS: They have gone to solid-state semiconductors instead of vacuum tubes. We use tubes for ease of service. Their sets are more reliable from what we can tell, but they do not offer the service that we do. Our designs are based around shortening the time for service. Their labor rates are a lot lower than ours.

Other businesses made similar statements, none of which had much to do with the problem. The foreign companies were succeeding in gaining market share because they had clear policies that caused work to be understood and accomplished throughout the corporation in the same way. Management took quality seriously; they listened to the workers; and they had reduced waste because they concentrated on properly using the resources they had. They did all this only because they had determined that these actions were necessary to overcome competition. This culture change did not come about because of a desire to be nice to everyone.

Each of the American industries affected had negative policies in these areas—or no policy at all. Most companies have not changed from that situation today; they are working harder and smarter but have not taken the aggressive and positive steps that result in a permanent culture change. The tone of an organization produces its result.

An Executive Mandate: Fostering Corporate Culture

If we are running a hot dog stand and produce dogs that are half cooked, placed on stale bread, and handed off with a snarl, we probably are going to have some difficulty getting repeat business. If the stand owner across the street has fresh buns, fully cooked dogs, free napkins, and service with a smile, he is probably going to clean our clock. Both stands have the same potential suppliers, the same source of employees, the same government regulation, the same customer base, and basically the same location. The difference is the culture that has been created within the organization—in this case, an organization of one.

American executives reacted to foreign competition with arrogance and blamed their functional departments for getting them into this situation. They also snarled that the customers did not understand how hard it was to produce the products and services that were being offered to them. The specialists had their own reasons:

> QUALITY: These people do not comply with industry quality level standards. They are trying to produce defect-free products and services, which is economically unsound. Therefore, they have to be selling below cost.

PURCHASING: They are able to make long-range deals with suppliers in order to get better prices. In many cases, they own part of the supplier. Our laws and procedures keep us from doing better. We have to get several bids and take the lowest one unless we have a wonderful reason, and we are not allowed to own part of a supplier although we can own it all.

PERSONNEL: Their people come to them well trained by the school system. They have no serious unions and no discipline problems. Also, they do not have to hire minorities regardless of qualifications. We have to do all our own training, and there are just not enough funds to do it all.

RESEARCH AND DEVELOPMENT: They get all the money they need as well as time to take our products and copy them. They can identify the problems we have had and design around them. We are always so busy with new things that we never have time for the older ones.

ENGINEERING: Our factories never produce what we design; there is never time to do it right. There is too much influence from marketing. They want so many gimmicks and so wide a line that we never can settle down to do what we would like to do.

FINANCE: There are too many demands for funds. Research and Development for instance, would take all of the capital budget if we would let them. We are not like these foreign firms who can get money for a small cost. We have to go to the market and dilute stock, or we have to borrow at prime plus. The manufacturing people want to continually upgrade their machinery before it is even written off. We would have to give up paying dividends in order to invest more.

MARKETING: We need to do more advertising to show our customers the advantages of buying American and staying loyal to our products. Our studies show that they would prefer to buy from us, but they are being pressured by what they perceive as lower costs and better quality. Actually, there is little difference between foreign products and our own, but it is hard to get that story out.

Others have the same line: "These people do not play according to GAOC" (generally accepted operating customs). In those GAOC situations it was only necessary to have quality, price, and delivery that was no worse than the competition. Serving the customer to the best of our ability had nothing to do with GAOCs. Customers routinely rotated among potential suppliers, changing when they were disappointed, and eventually working their way back around to the original vendors. So a Ford would be traded in on a Chevrolet, which would be swapped for a Plymouth after a few years. Then an exchange for a Ford would begin the cycle all over again. The eternal hope of buying something that performed as the advertisement promised drove the customer's part of the revolution. They were tired of being disappointed.

All of the reasons provided for the loss of market share and the destruction of the previously calm and predictable world of business seem to revolve around the inadequacies of people, the restrictions of operations, the unfair advantages of the competition, and the fickleness of the buying public. However, the real reason for this debacle, as well as the next one brewing on the horizon, *lies squarely in the hands of the executives.* They have been working hard—on the wrong things. They have not taken time to learn their jobs; they have not been taught the difference between an executive and a manager.

Thus, when a manager is promoted to an executive position, she or he waits for the telephone to ring or the mail to arrive or the boss to give direction. The problems or situations on the other end of these communications determine where attention is going to be directed. This means that the company is run by the wheels that make the most noise or have the most troubles. By the time the manager figures out that being an executive is different from what went on before, a pattern has been formed that is difficult to break.

An Executive Mandate: Creating Policy

Executives make things happen. Managers run those things. If executives pass their creative responsibilities downward, then what happens will be based on local needs rather than corporate objectives. This means that executives must concern themselves with policy.

Policy is not some archaic bit of brown paper hidden in leather-covered books positioned on everyone's credenza. Policy is what the organization does all the time. If none is established formally, then one will come forth on its own, based on the previous experience of those involved.

Here's an example. I like to pay bills as soon as I receive them. During my early years, it was not always easy to handle my diminutive cash flow on an uninterrupted basis. But I worked hard at it and managed to keep a good credit rating over the years, which allowed me to borrow money when I needed it in order to keep a good credit rating. Others may be able to relate to that. Now my cash flow has become more comfortable.

Recently, we (my wife and I) decided that the regular paying of personal bills was becoming time-consuming and boring, so we arranged with the trust department of a bank to pay them for us. We receive the bills, initial them, and forward the statements to the trust department. They make out the checks, send them off to the supplier, and give us a monthly record of what has transpired. We supply money for the account, send them the bills, and they do the rest.

However, soon after all this began, we started to get late notices and even a couple of dunning phone calls. When I asked the trust people about it, they stated that they saw no reason for paying before the float time was up since we were not a commercial account and did not get discounts for prompt payment. I told them that I wanted the bills paid within a day or two of their arrival at the bank. I also told them my reason.

The trust officer smiled and nodded, thanked me for the

direction, and we have never had a problem again. This was a clear case in which the executive (me) had neglected to give the policy to the manager (the trust officer) responsible for doing the job. Once that was accomplished, we were all on the same track. It would have been easy to just rant and rave, blaming the bank for hiring such thoughtless people, and perhaps change banks. Actually they were just conforming to the normal practice of their profession. Banks have zero imagination, they do whatever the others are doing.

Downtown Orlando, Florida, for instance, has seven new skyscrapers, all built in the past five years. Each of them is owned and/or occupied by a bank. Five of these buildings have bank names on them which begin with "First." The other two are old names. There is nothing wrong with this, of course, but it does say something about the direction of the executives.

Quality, finance, and relationships are the subjects that cover the policy waterfront. They also supply a full plate of activity for the executive in dealing with the past, present, and future. Nothing else is left.

Finance refers to the complete direction of the financial resources of the corporation, from acquiring funds through disbursing and managing them. It relates to personnel compensation, research—everything. Nothing happens unless a financial decision has been made and implemented.

Quality has to do with whether things are done properly or not. A professional football team, for instance, should never be off side at any time. This means they should never receive a penalty for lining up wrong or starting too soon. These people have spent their entire lives learning the complexities of their game. Not to be able to hold their place in formation is really sloppy, and no coach should tolerate it in himself or the players. Yet normal executive behavior is to accept such things as a routine part of business. Prevention must become the order of the day.

Relationships are where it all comes together or comes apart. Nothing else can be made to happen if relationships do not exist.

"No One Is Against the Right Things, but…"

A company is a complex entity, made more complex when it becomes larger. But even in the most intimate operation, the employees cannot sit at the side of their executive all day and ask for guidance. As the levels of communication deepen, direction becomes even more muddled. The executive's assumption that everything will be done to the satisfaction of the customer can become heavily diluted by a middle manager who wants all the trucks back in the garage by 4:30 P.M. regardless.

The desire to be debt free can be overcome by a comptroller whose experience has been in using a revolving line of credit rather than cash flow to pay suppliers. Keeping professionals up-to-date through their outside organizations can be muddled by the decision to stop paying their dues as part of the overall benefit package.

People can become disillusioned with the company when performance appraisals are no longer utilized regularly and promotions are determined solely by the personnel department. The establishment of parking spaces for "important" people can turn off those who are, consequently, made to feel unimportant. Products and services are supplied that do not meet the advertised requirements of the company because of schedule or cost conflicts. Managers make those decisions based on the events of the moment.

All of these are things that the executives probably would not want to happen if asked about it. No one is against the right things. However, unless someone states emphatically just what the "right things" are and are not, then others will use their judgments, which are inevitably based on a different agenda.

The interesting thing is that executives automatically develop and insist upon policies in time of great trouble. Upon taking over a sinking craft or business, the executive issues orders:

- "Hang on to the cash. Don't spend a cent until we see where we are."

- "Bring the asset list up to date. Let's see what we could sell without hurting the basic business."

- "Tell the customers that we are going to fulfill their orders and that the quality will be better than ever."

- "Calm the employees. We're going to have to cut back, but it will be done in a fair and equitable manner."

- "Get the banks together and let's agree on a way to refinance the operation."

- "Let's take an unbiased look at the market and see if our product line is what we really want. It may be necessary to acquire other lines and/or dump some of the ones we have."

Out of these commands and actions come policies. The customs that made the company "fat and uncompetitive" will disappear. The company will revert to being lean and mean, reversing the trends and going on to success. However, if the policies that caused the turnaround are not continually reinforced and upgraded, the culture that created the original situation will regenerate.

Relationships, quality, and finance—the next three chapters relate to each of these subjects. After discussing them in conceptual form, I will introduce five fictional vignettes in succeeding chapters in which an attempt is made to formalize the education of new executives. The cases are real-life in appearance, if not in actuality. If some of the characters seem recognizable, it is because of the reader's imagination, not my intent.

2
Relationships

The Organization as Ecosystem

The ecology of an organization is as delicate and vulnerable as that of a forest. This supports that; that feeds those; those dispense these, which in turn feed this. Any part of the life cycle that is disrupted or altered affects other parts, rarely for better, usually for worse. Nothing happens without having an effect on something. Sometimes the results will not be discernible for weeks, months, or years. Companies can be just as mysterious as forests. The key to all these things within a company, as within a forest, is relationships.

The Executive Responsibility for Relationships

The tone of organizational relationships is established by executives, directly or indirectly. Insensitive management can eliminate a forest just as proper direction can help it become glorious. Organizations glow or dim depending on how people perceive each other, how they work together, and how their actions interrelate. It is not a matter of money or education. After all, the really well-documented historical epics about unhappy people were conducted in palaces and mansions by people of extreme wealth and privilege. They had to work hard to make themselves miserable. Shakespeare's tragedies are all about overachievers and their problems. The popular soap operas, both daytime and prime time, are about folks who should know better. They seem to like tearing things apart.

Relationships are personal—between people. The way accounting and engineering get along has little to do with the systems or procedures of the company. It has everything to do with the tone people take with each other. It revolves around the empathy, or lack of it, that is projected by those who conduct the interface. One of the concerns of the executive is to take catalytic action when necessary. It is necessary to step in and strengthen relationships to get the job done properly. Situations cannot be neglected on the premise that they will work themselves out; they usually will not.

When I was the quality manager of Pershing at Martin back in the "Stone Age," the technical director of the program was the Army Ballistic Missile Agency (ABMA) located at Huntsville, Alabama. The leaders of ABMA (which later became a foundation of NASA) were the German rocket scientists who had been brought to the United States after World War II. Dr. Wernher Von Braun was the head of the organization.

ABMA was very concerned about quality in the development and production of this weapons system and assigned an entire laboratory to monitor the project. Their Quality and Reliability laboratory (Q&R lab) looked over my shoulder as quality manager, just as other labs kept an eye on parallel areas of the program. We had regular meetings with formal agendas, and they put two people in residence on site in Orlando. We were very concerned with keeping them happy and also appreciated the opportunity to learn from them. They wanted everything to succeed, particularly since this was their first involvement with a weapons system, at least with their present employer. Prior to that time they were working on space rockets and had developed those which put the first American satellites into orbit. It was an ABMA-designed vehicle that first put our astronauts into space. They knew what they were doing.

As the program progressed, we worked hard on the relationship, but it became apparent that everything was not smooth and sure. Someone in Huntsville would ask a question of the ABMA people in Orlando; they would relay the question to us and send the answer back. When we had our regular monthly meetings with the quality people of all areas, there was always a list of unanswered or not fully answered questions. This caused a lot of hassle. The ABMA people had their own intramural disagreements, and we often found ourselves caught in between. Also, the Martin people did not always know what to reveal and what to keep inside. Repeated direction that we would willingly share *everything* did little to overcome the communication gridlock. Mistrust was apparent, even though everyone knew that we were all of good will.

My evaluation was that the key to the problem rested in the various departments inside the Q&R lab. They all needed information and resented having to relay questions through the local ABMA people, who did not always consider the questions important enough to act on at that moment. If they called Martin directly, they usually got the wrong person or were refused an answer until clearance had been obtained. There was a great deal of frustration among all hands.

So I asked one of our senior quality department people, Bob Vincent, to go live in Huntsville. Bob, kicking and screaming but dutiful, moved his family and agreed to stay two years. His assignment was to sit at a desk in the Q&R lab and help people get their questions answered. He had authority to call anyone at Martin and complete the transaction. He also had the responsibility of making certain that the proper Martin and ABMA people knew what was happening. Bob's expenses came from the Quality Department overhead budget and were not part of the contract itself. Not everyone thought this was a wonderful idea, particularly the local ABMA representatives. Bob, who hated to leave Florida even for a moment, was not too thrilled with it either.

However, the improvement was immediate. Bob, who was recognized as being without guile and who knew everyone at Martin, began to be utilized right away. For instance, someone working on the soldering procedure asked him about Martin's training program. Bob made a call while the person stood beside the desk, and soon the proper people were helping each other. The information about this particular transaction was passed along, and the result was a working group on soldering. No problems surfaced from that area thereafter.

The flight-test program schedule needed attention, and Bob joined the ABMA people in a trip to Cape Canaveral to settle matters.

Bob talked to me several times a week, and I reported to the project director and quality director what he was doing. There were dozens of interfaces each week. During the two years he was in Huntsville, Bob never succumbed to the typical "field-representative syndrome" of switching allegiance away from the home team. When he left Huntsville, he was given a big party and his successor was welcomed. However, enough people now knew their communication counterparts and enough animosity had disappeared to allow operations to run smoothly after that. After a while, there was no need for a "resident catalytic agent." This was not always true in other laboratory relationships.

The point is that here was a case where systems, organizations, procedures, contracts, and other forms of conflict were set aside as everyone dealt with a person they trusted. This trust and eagerness spread through the organization as the realization developed that both sides were interested only in making a highly reliable weapons system within the budget and on time. And that, in fact, was the result.

An Executive Mandate: Mastering a Multitude of Relationships

Solving the problems of relationships is not always so direct and manageable. We often do not realize how many people we need to work with in order to run our lives. During a recent business trip, I decided to keep track of all the people-interface experiences that came my way. After counting 34 exchanges by noon, I gave it up as an administrative job I was not prepared to handle. Travel, for the most part, is a realm in which strangers comply with some generally accepted but unspoken rules of courtesy and communication. The encounters en route to the destination typically consume minimum amounts of time and usually have some purpose, such as buying a ticket or newspaper, registering for a room, asking directions, getting another cup of coffee, or having casual conversations with fellow travelers.

Such activities do not really qualify as personal relationships since they usually are not ongoing. Conversely, some of my most informative conversations have developed through chance encounters on airplanes or other forms of public transportation. It is amazing what people will tell total strangers when there is nothing else to do. Also I have acquired a few clients as a result of those impromptu sessions.

I try not to be any trouble while traveling, or while doing anything else for that matter. If people are difficult, there is no reason for responding in kind and thus adding one more ingrate to the world's supply. If a trip is not going to be useful and rewarding, then there is no use taking it. Travel should be a continuation of normal life, not some special situation.

Arriving at my business destination places me in a whole different world. I will be where they expect me, they know me or about me, and the situation is friendly. They are looking forward to something happening and have opinions about it all. If the purpose of my presence is to meet with a large group, make a speech, answer questions, and offer some fellowship, then the attitude of the group will be determined by my attitude. If I am pleasant, they will be pleasant. If I am hostile, they will be hostile.

Those who arranged the session will be nervous, wanting to assure that it comes out positively. (Sometimes I greet them whispering hoarsely that I have had a little throat trouble and might be unable to speak. However, this is like pulling wings off flies and does not reflect a good attitude on my part.) The organizers will want to make certain that the important people in their organization are met and appreciated by the guest, and that everyone is properly entertained and stimulated.

My responsibility, outside of presenting as entertaining and stimulating a program as possible, is to be pleasant and not require too much help. Most of this is accomplished by the advance planning of the day to ensure arriving well rested, in plenty of time, and well prepared. We will have arranged for a room if one is necessary and know something about the people who are "renting" me.

Audiences have personalities. Veteran speakers know that they have to identify that personality and mesh with it immediately if they are going to be thought entertaining and stimulating. They cannot just reel out the same old standard talk each time. Since this relationship has only a few moments to become established, it is necessary to see the stage and its arrangement, ask if the brief biography for the introduction was received, and, in general, eliminate as many "land mines" as possible.

Consulting visits are different. Here we enter a world of permanent people who have their own agendas, problems, and opinions. Companies have personalities, but management teams do not. Each member sees the group differently, and although they act in a common cause, their reasons usually are different. Many times separate factions are operating, not necessarily about things of great importance, but not everyone agrees on everything. Only outsiders can see the invisible lines; to insiders there appears to be consistent fellowship.

Establishing Lines of Communication and Keeping Them Open

Some "purposeful conflict" is necessary for success, I suspect, but it can waste a lot of time if the purposefulness is not properly contained. That is why I like to get teams to develop at least a common language on management. It is necessary to establish relationships with the team as a whole and with the members as individuals. Mutual understanding reveals what everyone wants to accomplish, and that leads to establishing requirements. When requirements exist, it is possible to determine what the relationship is all about and get everything on a practical basis. Establishing all this only with the executives is not enough; it is also necessary to create communication with the company as a whole.

Many management teams live with delusion: things are not what they think they are. On a recent visit, I was led on a two-hour tour of the entire location, then brought back to the conference room where the management team was assembled. The general manager launched into a discussion about the effectiveness of the team and at one point commented on the excellent relationship they had with all the employees.

I interrupted to note that I had just been led past every employee in the organization and introduced to none of them. I commented that to me this did not communicate that they much cared for their employees. (I realize that this sounds like I was being less than courteous, but it is necessary to move a group out of its normal rhythm if we are going to get anywhere.) This remark was met with nods of agreement from half the group and stares of disbelief from the other half. The general manager smiled, blushed a little, and allowed that my observation was probably correct given the evidence. The subject of the meeting changed from trying to impress me with their management competence to having a profitable, open discussion on improvement. He introduced me to his secretary on the way out. She was pleasantly surprised.

The story of what went on in that conference room leaked to the rest of the organization almost immediately; and, as a result, we had the chance to establish a proper relationship with the employees of that company. When that company began its quality education effort, it was received with an excellent attitude by the personnel at all levels. And that is the purpose of positive and meaningful relationships: to smooth company operations and produce satisfaction for everyone. The "meaningful" part of positive and meaningful relationships comes from the genuine desire of each person to make things work. Almost everything that does not work got that way because of a relationship problem somewhere in its cycle.

Corporation—Family Parallels

It is common for parents and children to have inadequate relationships. Even though they love each other, they do not always get along well. The causes of conflict with a loved one are very complex and beyond the scope of this book. However, such causes are usually rooted in who is or is not in charge of what and whom. People have deep needs to be respected, particularly by those whom they love. They have long antennae that monitor such feelings continually.

It is quite uncommon, however, for grandparents and grandchildren to have relationship problems. They get along just fine—perhaps, as someone has said, because they have common enemies. But the main reason they do so well is that they want to please each other, and very little is permitted to get in the way of that. Grandparents put up with a lot and say very little. Grandchildren behave better because they do not have to work so hard to get what they want. They are under no pressure to compete for love, attention, and resources. As long as the parents remember not to wear the older people out, this is one of the more solid relationships of life.

That we live in a world where relationships are important is obvious, but like many obvious things, we do not necessarily understand or do them well. The basis of much unhappiness can be found in absence of relationships, and that has been so since the beginning of recorded history. We see families disintegrating on a regular basis; we see companies, suppliers, and customers unable to work with each other. We see groups, tribes, political entities, nations, and all kinds of assemblages unable to get along. Wars rarely happen between people with a common understanding of goals and purposes.

"No Company Is an Island"

Just "getting along" in itself would be significant progress in many social and political situations, but that is not enough when it comes to running a corporation properly. Relationships within corporate life must be created purposefully and monitored continually. They are the source of the affirmative structures capable of supporting life. Companies, like people, cannot live long when their insides are not working together. Lungs and kidneys cannot go off in different directions for very long before something undesirable begins to occur. When employees continually find out about company actions through the newspapers rather than hearing it up front and personally, they feel amputated. Try that with *feet*.

Nations can decide to disagree and still be around when the pouting ends. Couples have been known to go years without speaking, after which they are both still alive, if mute. However, the business world does not possess such a tolerance level. Either a company does what is expected, or it is cut off from intercourse—and it cannot live all by itself. There is no announced plan along this line; it just happens. No company is an island, as the poet came close to saying. Companies would have a difficult time surviving without suppliers, customers, participating employees, or financial sources. Contacts with all those entities must be nurtured and treasured, or they will dry up and wither. Sometimes atrophied limbs can be rubbed back to life, but they never are as useful as before.

To have a better grasp of the scope we are assigning to the

word "relationship," let us look at a sample of some of relationships that the executive must accept as a personal concern.

Internal

- **Executives with each other.** Are they willing to support each other by actions?
- **Executives with managers and employees.** Do they have enough empathy to understand and help people do their jobs? Do they listen? Do they develop? Do they give permission to do the jobs right?
- **Executives with their personal staffs.** Is loyalty respected? Are workers treated with respect? Are they given knowledge?
- **Managers with senior people.** Do they take time to understand requirements and contribute to their development? Are they loyal and helpful?
- **Managers with junior people.** Do they take enough interest to make certain that proper training and attention is given to people? Do they build a "family" environment?
- **Employees with each other and with seniors.** Do they reach out to help meet the company objectives? Are they interested in growing? Do they trust the management?

External

- **Customers.** Do they feel we know their needs and try to meet them? Do they have someone they can talk to? Do they pay promptly?
- **Suppliers.** Do they have the opportunity to help us improve? Do they feel we buy on a cost only basis? Do they respect us? Do they have someone to talk to?
- **Community.** Do they know we are here? Do they know

what we do? Do we receive proper services? Do we have a
community-relations program?

- **Competition.**   Do others in our business think well of us?
Do we have access to all pertinent information? Do we
know what the future looks like?
- **Financial sources.**   Do they know our business and people? What do they think of us?

Family

- **Spouse.**   Does the spouse understand the business requirements and agree to the amount of dedication involved? Are
the benefits as clear as the detriments?
- **Children.**   Do they know where the executive goes? Have
they been there? Do they receive enough personal attention—weekends at least? Is there basic communication?
Does the family eat together regularly?
- **Other family members.**   Is there regular contact?
- **Faith.**   Is the family led to church by the executive? Does
the family discuss their faith openly? Do they practice it?

Taking Relationships As They Come

Not all relationships are formally generated. While on a recent skiing trip, I tried to pass a large delivery truck on the
snowy road near our rented house. This was not one of my
better ideas as I soon became hopelessly sunk in the snow
bank. The four-wheel-drive vehicle just spun all four tires.
Fortunately, the house was only a couple of hundred yards
away; and I walked there, called for a tow truck, and was
pleased to learn that they not only knew my ditch, but would
be there in five minutes. That gave me just enough time to
walk back.

The truck arrived moments after I did. I asked the driver

what he wanted me to do and soon was sitting behind the wheel, engine in neutral, prepared to steer. He looked the job over, shoveled some snow from under the front of the car, hooked up a cable, and pulled me out. I paid him for his work, gave him my thanks, and we both went our ways. But I have a warm spot for him and for his company. They did what they told me they would do, when they said they would do it, and the man did not make any snide remarks about my being stuck in the snow. He didn't even smirk. I liked that.

Now we have a relationship. Here is someone who can be trusted. I do not plan to ask him to execute my estate or join us for Thanksgiving dinner, but he is on my list of people who know what they are doing. How many people do we know personally who know what they are doing? It is up to the executive to find them and make certain that they can exist happily in the organization. No one else is going to arrange this. Personnel departments have no way of telling who can do a job and who can't.

Conclusion

The executive has to be assertive and deliberate about managing the ecology of the operation. Doing that requires knowing what is going on and taking relationships seriously—long-range. No organization or forest can grow and prosper based on a series of temporary, stop-gap measures. People need to know where they stand and what is going on under the ground.

3
Quality

Weaving Quality into the Corporate Fabric

Executives worry about quality, in one way or another, more than anything else. "How is this doing?" "How is that working out?" "Are customers happy with our new offering?" The subject of quality encompasses the entire spectrum of the company. Every action taken by every employee involves quality. Most of the conversations held at the executive level concern things that have gone wrong, seem to be going wrong, or might go wrong. There is a lot of wondering about why things do not go righter and how all that could be changed.

Various techniques and systems have been offered over the years to handle the enigma of quality. Each works to some degree and each has its advocates. However, none really makes much difference because these conventional approaches do not require that quality become the basic policy of the company. One would think that executives and quality professionals would wise up to the fact that these techniques have not been effective all by themselves for 50 years. But many keep hoping that they can find a substitute for managerial attention and hard work.

Quality is the result of a carefully constructed culture; it has to be the fabric of the organization—not part of the fabric, but the actual fabric. It is really not very hard for a modern management team to produce quality if they are willing to learn how to change and implement. However, it is not as simple as adopting a few tools or techniques. Those who bought robots or hung up charts to overcome quality problems learned they were just creating more expensive mistakes.

An Executive Mandate: Wiping the Slate Clean

To begin with, the operating field must be swept clean of contradictory personal agendas and goals. In the real world, although it is difficult to believe, not everyone is for quality. Sometimes it can seem like a good idea to have everything in turmoil to provide the opportunity of becoming famous by constructing a turnaround. Some people really think like that. Making a mess and then getting credit for cleaning it up is still an effective way of getting ahead, particularly when management has few accurate and realistic measurements.

The Foundation of Quality: "A Few Understandings"

Quality is really the least difficult of the three concerns of executives to attack and overcome. There is a great deal of evidence showing that change can be accomplished without spending much money or inflicting a great deal of pain. The solution comes down to a few understandings.

Conformance to Requirements

First, everyone needs to agree that quality means "conformance to requirements" and that management's prime responsibility is to cause the right requirements to be created. People need to know what their jobs are, what they are expected to do, and how all this is going to be measured. Management must explain in a way that people cannot misunderstand what the product or service is to be and what needs to go on within the organization. The people have to be able to turn that understanding into work that produces the desired result. Marketers have to make certain that the real needs of the customers are being met. Services performed must be exactly what the advertisement said they would be.

Prevention

Second, all action must be oriented around prevention. Each person must know the content of his or her job and be trained to accomplish it. Measurements must be used to determine the continual need for improvement and resources dedicated to that. Managers who learn to think in a preventive manner should be rewarded and recognized.

Companywide Commitment

Third, the policy of the company must be that every individual will understand the requirements of his or her job and will conform to them. No deviations will be permitted. Management must insist on this. Otherwise, management does not run the company. They will spend their time making up plans and actions that no one executes. Others will routinely decide that this or that is "good enough," and inadequate services or products will be provided to the customers.

When quality is defined as conformance to requirements, "goodness" has nothing to do with it. There is no room for "quality levels"; everything must be accomplished as promised. Then people can depend on each other. Management must establish a quality policy that says "We will deliver defect-free products and services, on time, to our customers, both internal and external."

Many big companies supported "quality control" departments and activities over the years and yet ran into big problems. They had a hard time understanding how that could be. Unfortunately, the basic concept of quality control is containment. It is based on "acceptable quality levels" which allow that a certain minimum of things be wrong. That attitude needs changing forever.

Measuring Noncompliance

Fourth, lack of compliance to these concepts and policies must be measured in financial terms as well as in customer satisfaction. Not doing things properly costs a great deal of money. Manufacturing companies spend 25 percent and more of their revenues on repair, warranty, scrap, excess inventory, overtime, and such. Service companies spend about half of their operating costs on similar things. Every time someone has to run up to a hotel room to deliver towels, it costs. When a person's name is spelled wrong on an insurance policy, it has to be fixed. Five or six people can be involved in these seemingly minor incidents. Things like this go on continually in service organizations. At any given moment half the people are doing old work. Just see how many are walking the aisles on their way to or from fixing something that was done wrong the first time.

A Health-Care Case

"Not a Hospital, but a 'Health-Care Boutique'"

Let's drop in on Harold Tomplinson, the president and chief executive of a health-care unit. It used to be called a hospital, but as Harold was saying, "There are not any hospitals any more; they have all become 'health-care boutiques.' The beds are half-full all the time, and patients do not stay long when they are put in them. We have all these separate units."

At this point he pulled a folded brochure from his coat pocket, opened it to a map of the facility, and laid it on the table.

"See, here is the outpatient department, our busiest area. Over here is the diagnostic clinic. Below the main building we have a group of smaller buildings for the wellness center, cancer center, emergency room, and the cardiac care unit. We also do same-day surgical operations.

"Patients come in, get treatment, go home. It is a completely new way of doing things and, generally, is much more efficient, too. Also, it usually is a lot easier for the patient, although I suspect that in some cases, the families would be just as glad to have them here where we can look after them instead of at home confusing things."

Facing the Music

Later that day at the trustees' meeting, as Harold went through his status report, one of the trustees asked him to comment on why the cash retention was falling off. (Not-for-profit health-care units do not talk about profit, they have "retained cash.") In this case, what would be called margin in other businesses was shrinking. The operation still was running in the black, but it was becoming much more of a challenge.

The financial officer explained to the Board that the government and the insurance companies now paid less per case than they did before. It was necessary to become more efficient in order to reduce costs. The medical staff, at the same time, was concerned about court decisions concerning malpractice, and the resulting increases in insurance premiums. They tended to overdo the diagnostic work.

"So," said one trustee, "while the revenues are decreasing, the doctors are ordering more tests and other services to avoid being accused of delinquency. Since most patients are under fixed payment arrangements, we have to learn to treat them within those boundaries. Right?"

"Right," said the head of the medical staff. "We are allowed a specific amount of money to treat a specific condition. If everything is done just so, and the condition cooperates, we can make it all come out. However, if the patient does not respond as planned, or someone does something wasteful, or a physician is overly cautious, then the whole thing winds up in the red."

Another trustee spoke up.

"Are you saying that financial considerations and limitations can override medical procedure and needs? That would be a sorry state. It would also probably be illegal."

The president shook his head.

"No, it is not that bad. However, the staff has to be aware that we do not have the bottomless-pit situation we had for years. In those days we spent what it took. And today, we still do what is necessary, but we do have to recognize the realities of life."

Another trustee smiled at the discussion.

"I can appreciate the concern, but you folks are always complaining about how someone has made it difficult for you. If we take a look at where we spend money and where we have increasing expenses, most of them are in the nonprofessional areas. For instance, if we look at this thick financial report you put out each month, it is apparent that we have a large accounts receivable overdue, and it is growing. Funding that is an expense that has nothing to do with the medical problems. It is strictly an administrative problem."

"Absolutely," said the president. "We have a lot of trouble in that area. It is really symptomatic. As you know, the health-care business has changed dramatically in the past few years. It is really incredible that in an industry this size—over 600 billion dollars in the United States alone—everyone is having trouble staying alive, let alone making any money. I think we would all be delighted just to break even."

"But all the solutions and concern seem to be directed at the medical side of the business," said the trustee. "I think no one has done much about the administrative part. For instance, concentrating only on the fees involved in delivering a baby may make us forget the number of administrative actions that come into play. A lot of paper shuffling goes on in insurance companies, the government, plus our operation here. The costs involved in all those people and systems working on getting us paid for that baby have to be more than the check is written for. The straight medical side is only a part of the package."

"And," said another trustee, "that is just if the job is done right the first time. Let's ask our comptroller. Just how often is one of these transactions completed without having to backtrack on it or write someone, or call or something? What is the rate of problems?"

The comptroller shrugged his shoulders.

"I don't have any certain numbers on it, but my guess would be that there is some problem or question with about half the claims. It can be that the doctor did not complete some line properly. (They hate these forms.) It could be that the patient did not provide the right information. (People get a little hyper when they are being admitted.) It could be that the hospital classified the case improperly; it could be that the claim was sent to the wrong place; it could be that the government changed the rules on something; it could be that someone in the insurer's office had a bad day and decided just to toss everything out. The permutations are infinite."

"All correct," said the president. "There will be a lot of talk about regulating physician's fees and lab tests and such, but all that will make little difference in the end. Our real problem is that we are awash in a mass of paperwork that no one really understands in total."

"In our company we define all of that as a problem with quality," said the trustee.

"We have a quality assurance department," remarked the comptroller. "Should they be getting into all this?"

"That is not the kind of quality I mean. The problem is not a medical or even a technical one. People start right off going after the medical professionals; it's like manufacturing companies going after the workers. Heaven knows, they have their troubles, but that is not where all the costs and waste lie. Most of it comes from the administrative and support areas."

The president was startled. He sat up in his chair and gave the trustee his full attention.

"But the costs of medical care are what is going up. Surely we must face that!"

"The costs go up because they have to pay for all the thrown away money."

The president bristled.

"I think 'thrown away' is a little strong. This is a very complicated situation. We certainly don't 'throw away' things on purpose."

The trustee was unrelenting.

"I accept that. Nonetheless, health-care costs are rising faster than inflation and faster than the costs of improved technology. Quality is the primary reason, or should I say lack of it."

The president settled back in his chair and pondered all this. When members of a usually cooperative board began to rumble at the chief executive, it was time for a little bit of listening.

"Let's start over. Perhaps I don't understand what you're saying when you talk about quality. We consider ourselves a quality operation, and we have been rated that way by every agency or organization that has had anything to do with us. Why do you think we have problems in this area?"

"Do you have a *policy* on quality?" ask the first trustee. "Where does management stand on this subject?"

"Certainly we have a policy," said the president. "We always let everyone know that we expect to be the highest-quality health-care operation possible. Everyone knows that."

The trustee shook his head.

"I mean a written policy that we teach the people and enforce every day. I have never seen one in all the material we receive here on the Board."

The president looked blank.

"I've always assumed that quality was a given, that people just naturally tried to do their best and that the company really didn't have to say much about it. On reflection, that might have been a misconception."

He rose to his feet and stood behind his chair.

"What you're saying," he addressed the trustees, "is that we actually have to get in and make quality happen? I have never thought of it like that. I need some more information on this. I think I'm beginning to like the idea. Where would I go to learn what to do?"

The trustee smiled and reached in his briefcase for a copy of a book on the subject.

"This book explains the logic of quality management and will get you started, but the organization is going to need formal help. Our company went to the Quality College."

The president accepted the book but still had a dubious expression and stance.

"Health care is not like manufacturing. There are a lot of individual decisions to be made every day, in administration as well as medicine. This is not an assembly line where people do the same things over and over. I'm not sure it is practical for us."

The trustee snorted.

"In the first place, only 15 percent of the people in my company ever touch the product, which is probably not much different than here, the product being the patient. In the second place, there are very few assembly lines anymore. Everyone is in some niche that does not permit much repeatability."

"Besides," said the second trustee, "we don't know at this moment just what areas are having problems. That is going to require a study. But you have already done some things along this line."

"Such as?" asked the president.

"Such as housekeeping. This place is immaculate and always has been. It is in better shape than any health-care operation I have ever seen—in fact, better than any public building I know of."

"Well, we insist on excellent housekeeping," said the president. "It is something that is very important to the health of the patients, to the morale of the staff, and to the image of the hospital."

"And how do you make it happen?"

"Like I said, we insist on it. Everyone knows they are expected to maintain a clean work space; we provide the resources; and the rules of housekeeping are posted all around the building, tastefully, of course. An employees' committee inspects the operation on a regular basis, chastising those who are sloppy and recognizing those who do well."

The trustees nodded in unison.

"That is what quality management is all about. Set clear requirements, teach people to understand them, provide the tools, and insist on compliance. Here you've been doing it all the time, and you didn't know it."

"You're saying that we don't have clear requirements for the people in other areas of operation? That we let them or the process set its own quality levels? I think you may have something there. We are going to take charge of this quality business. I really appreciate your helping me understand this."

Sound like a familiar scenario? Here's how one organization went about changing the picture.

Contributing Factors to Malaise

When the health-care management team conducted an analysis of individual operations, they discovered that errors and other nonconformances were part of the normal life of the organization. The laboratories routinely lost samples, sent reports to the wrong areas, obtained inconsistent results, and had sloppy filing procedures. All this was blamed on lack of trained personnel, inconsiderate doctors who always wanted things rushed, and the general sense of the times.

Nurses and doctors were found to be not following the agreed administrative procedures and were taking shortcuts where they felt them necessary. This, they felt, was their prerogative, and they were not interested in taking the time to officially change the procedures to what was really workable.

The accounting office was so convinced that the paying institutions were going to search each application for some reason to delay payment that they did not take seriously proper completion of the forms. They waited until the paperwork was rejected, then corrected it according to the complaints. This only happened in about 30 percent of the cases, but it was enough to double the size of the department. There was no effort underway to smooth out the payment cycle.

Purchasing had increased the inventory by 60 percent over the past 18 months. Because of various shortages that had occurred, purchasing had been severely criticized, and one buyer had been terminated. They vowed never to run out of anything again, so items were ordered as far in advance as possible. The thoughts of going to a "just-in-time" delivery system brought peals of laughter from the purchasing agents. Management, they said, would never permit such a thing. All they (management) were interested in was getting everything as cheaply as possible and never being out of what was needed. The thought that working on relationships and quality could accomplish all this was something that could not be sold at that time.

So the attitude that nothing could be done to make things happen properly was binding the entire organization. People spent time going *around* the system because the system was known not to work; departments built defensive walls to protect themselves from the incompetence of other areas—all of this in an operation which was considered by its peers to be an example of efficiency and dedication. Management sailed blithely along, steering through channels, around shoals, and avoiding boulders, all the while convinced that they were carrying out their assigned tasks in grand fashion. It never dawned on them that operations could be better.

Introducing a Process for Change

Policy. Once a "do it right the first time" policy on quality was established, and education was initiated to explain exactly what that policy meant, things began to change. The lab people began to look into the causes of samples being lost, mislaid, or confused. They found that there was not a standard, well-understood way of identifying the samples at the time they were taken. They determined that the handling flow had never been spelled out. It became clear that test methods were not standardized, that technicians were using their own experience rather than an agreed-on procedure. Everyone became positive about eliminating the possibility of error. The doctors became cooperative after one technician revealed that workers had to go to the doctor's lounge every day and look through the pockets of discarded white coats to retrieve forgotten lab-test requests.

Finance. The financial people took another look at cash flow, especially accounts receivable, and learned that a large "float" existed. Several millions of dollars were unavailable for use because of delays in the system. Discussions with the insurance firms led to a fax-and-wire transfer arrangement that let most claims be faxed from the health-care unit to the insurance company in an agreed format. This resulted in funds being wire transferred to the bank within 48 hours. Similar arrangements with suppliers led to the hospital's receiving discounts on its purchases for paying promptly. All of this promptly relieved stress in the financial system.

Employee Input. Personnel of all levels learned to communicate with each other. They introduced an "error-cause-removal" system that let people send management a clear message about the things that kept them from doing their jobs right the first time. As a result, procedure committees were formed in various areas to document agreements of the proper ways of doing things. Since they had a large hand in developing these procedures, the personnel joyfully conformed to them. This reduced the amount of confusion and error in the professional areas. Doctors began to treat other professionals with more consideration because what they were doing became more predictable and less confusing.

Cultural "Healing." As these culture changes became part of normal operations, the entire business became much more profitable, much less trouble, and more satisfying in terms of working conditions. Employee turnover dropped to the lowest level ever, and employee grievances all but disappeared. No one took this for granted. They all kept working at it because they liked the atmosphere that was generated. They could depend on each other.

The Executive Role

The educational material and technical support that generated this change came from professional people who develop and provide that as their business in life. It came from outside the hospital. But the actions that made it all happen were the direct result of executive policy and direction. Most of the changes occurred within a year. From that time on improvement was a continual consideration. Recognition programs were begun and other health-care operations began to visit in order to gain some knowledge about how to do it all. Imagine becoming famous, models in the field, just by learning how to do properly what you are supposed to do anyway.

All of this improvement was based on prevention. The entire field of health care could benefit from this thought. In a financially strapped and troubled health world, executives need to learn that reducing the price of curing a patient is not where the solution lies. Preventing people from becoming ill is the only way to bring the situation under control.

The most expensive diseases, such as those involving the heart, are mostly preventable. A fraction of the money spent on heart-bypass surgery could educate and assist people in not having the problems in the first place.

Toward a Quality Tomorrow?

The same concepts apply to all other businesses. As the executive establishes the ecology of the organization, prevention has to become an actual, integral part of policy. Today, it is a desirable goal that is considered unattainable. Yet all the knowledge required to make it happen exists. Sailors suffered from beriberi and scurvy long after it was known that fruit juice would prevent it. Packing away a few boxes of lemons takes care of the problem. But some captains resented being told what to do.

Surely none of that breed is left?

4

Finance

How to Recognize and Sidestep Financial "Black Holes"

Black holes are places way out in the universe where the magnetic concentration is so strong that even light cannot escape. The earth, it is said, would concentrate into the size of a basketball if it were to become a black hole. This is a situation from which there is no apparent escape given the resources that we now know about.

There is virtually no possibility, at least with what we know now, that any of us will ever become personally involved with a celestial black hole. Very few of them appear on the way to grandma's house or even to work. However, the financial world, both professional and personal, is a forest of actual and potential "black holes" with magnetic strength sufficient to easily overcome an individual or a business. It is not an equal contest or a fair one. Those who would direct the life of an organization or a family should be very aware of these seductive, yet deadly, phenomena. We must not overestimate our instinctive ability to identify "black holes" early in their formative stages and thus evade them. Getting drawn into one always seems like the easiest thing to do at the time, but these "tar pits" contain the bones of many financially sophisticated people.

Remember Your First "Black Hole"?

My first personal "black-hole" experience occurred around the time I was in the sixth grade. One day as I was walking home from school, a man called several of us over to his car and asked if we wanted to earn some money. We were to become salespeople for his magazines which included several well-known names of that day: *Liberty, Colliers, Popular Mechanics,* and a few others.

If we would go door to door and get people to take subscriptions, we could win baseball gloves and other prizes. It sounded like a good deal to me, so I gave him my name and address, took the attractive sack containing several sample magazines, learned how to fill out the order book, and went on my way. My father was thrilled that I was finally showing some signs of being interested in making money. My mother was not so sure. My brother suggested that if I wanted a glove, I should ask our grandfather for one. (My brother always was the most practical of the family.)

During the next week I was able to get six neighbors to sign up for magazines. When the man reappeared, I handed him the order forms and asked him how much more was involved before I got the glove. He looked at me in amazement. "Where's the money?" he asked. "I don't need just order blanks. People are supposed to give you the money, too. You owe me twelve dollars."

In one stroke I had been transformed from a carefree, grade-school boy to a world-class debtor. Thoughts of debtor's prison and other Dickensian lifestyles immediately flashed before my eyes. Twelve dollars was a sum beyond my comprehension. My grandmother put 10 cents a week in Christmas clubs for my brother and me. She would trudge to the bank every Wednesday, make her deposit, and return

home. That five dollars took care of all my Christmas shopping and gave me the opportunity to buy a special friend
something sweet. Twelve dollars was two and a half years at
10 cents a week. I didn't see how I could have gotten that far
behind in just a few days.

When I went back to my customers for the money, they
each said that they expected to pay once they saw the magazines coming in. The man said that no magazines would be
coming until he saw the money. He offered to let me off the
hook for six dollars, saying that I could keep the other six
after I collected. He could begin the subscriptions for six, although he would make no profit himself. There would be no
glove. (My brother was looking smarter all the time.)

After a week of sleepless nights, I finally told my father
what was going on. He went with me to see the man, who after an earnest and somewhat one-sided discussion, tore up
the subscription slips and promised never to come around
again. That was the only time I ever saw my father angry. He
made me go back to the potential subscribers and tell them
that the deal was off.

From that point on, whenever I became involved in any
sort of business or financial activity, my father would remind
me of this adventure. And, in truth, I have had much more
serious exposures, primarily because I am an incurable opti-
mist. I always think things are going to work out, or go on
forever, or whatever it is that makes one see the best side of
anything. But I have never disappeared completely into a
black hole because of such experiences. I at least learned that
I had to take care of myself and understand any deal completely before becoming involved. My father would not be
able to bail me out again. This is the way we learn.

Manufacturing Financial Malaise

Scenes from a Marriage.   In a sense, financial black holes
seem to be a part of the scenery. Young couples, for instance,
have a sort of rite of passage that requires them to manage

their money in the first couple of years in a way that places them in debt over their heads. Then along comes a baby, or another, similar situation arises, and one of them has to quit working. Suddenly they are in trouble because of the need for two incomes. They borrow in order to meet current needs, but to no avail. Unless some caring relative bails them out, they are caught in this "black hole" for years until revenue finally catches up with, and passes, expenses—if it ever does. The only positive aspect of this condition is that they cannot afford a divorce.

These are bright young people who have been counseled on sex, relationship, health care, careers, and virtually everything else except how to stay out of debt while living well. It all happens so fast. Neither of them wants to irritate the new mate by bringing up the subject of financial management and getting specific on who will spend what for what. They usually do not even talk much about casual debt such as comes with credit cards. They will talk about a house if that is in the picture. By the time they realize that speaking is necessary, it may well have become shouting.

An Entrepreneurial Blowout.   Organizations have the same opportunities for generating "black holes." A young friend of mine started a company to manufacture a product of his own design. I was very impressed with it and felt that it had a good future. He received an order from a distributor and wanted to borrow 150 thousand dollars to buy the material to deliver a year's supply to the buyer. Since he had no credit, he asked me to cosign a note at the bank. I suggested that he did not really need to do a whole year's worth at once; and that if the buyer would give him a contract, the bank would be happy to lend him enough to make a couple of month's worth. Then he would have no long-term debt and could be in business with little effort. (The Bible notes that you do no one a favor if you enable them to obtain a loan that their situation will not permit a prudent banker to make.)

But the purchasing company would have no part of that, so he and his parents took out second mortgages on their homes and got the money. The buyer never provided a contract and never paid anything. Now they are trying to build a business with no money because it takes everything that comes in to pay off the home loans. We were able to help him find an equity investor to bail him out, but it cost him control of his company. With patience he could have been rich; now he is working for a salary with the potential of being well off some day. Rich is better.

An Executive Mandate: Staying One Up on Financial Issues

Patience and discretion are the keys to not being trapped in a "black hole." It also helps to know exactly where all the money is coming from and where it is going. Many executives do not keep up-to-date on the components of their cash flow.

This sort of approach is an invitation to disaster as testified by the large percentage of startups that fail. Most of those attribute lack of success to not having enough capital, but that is usually not the case. Debt servicing, money-losing functions, and a poor usage of cash flow are usually the culprits. New companies traditionally hire an accounting firm to "do their books" on a regular basis, which they do after the fact. Organizations with larger revenues and cash flow will get a bookkeeper to keep track of transactions and chase after the overdue bills while holding vendors off as long as possible. The big companies have formal and complicated finance departments but often keep the data secret.

In these kinds of environments management is always working behind the financial curve. It is not possible to have a budget system that controls what is being spent, only one that shows what was disbursed. The boss feels fairly comfortable because no one can get hired without everyone knowing about it, and no big expenditures can be made without a check being presented for signature. But that is not where the money leaks. The startup executive needs to handle each penny personally in order to know where it came from and

where it is planned to go. Money should only be spent for
life-essential activities. Anything not necessary to keep the
body working should be postponed.

Large companies with large accounting departments have
computerized reporting and conduct formal budget preparation sessions. Each level of management has a definition of
what it is permitted to spend, and each management meeting
features a discussion of the financial status of the organization. Every department or other entity is shown to be on, behind, or ahead of its separate budget. The boss gets a feeling
of confidence from all this that comes from all the columns
of figures adding up correctly.

Yet even these companies are continually running into problems, such as being surprised by unplanned expenses or lack of
revenues. These result in an embarrassed announcement that
disappoints those who follow the company. Managerial actions
are usually drastic in such a case and often result in laying off
people, cutting back on projects, and borrowing money. All of
this creates turmoil inside the company and takes management's eyes off running the organization.

Managing finance is often considered an overhead function that does not contribute directly to profitability. Inter-
estingly enough, the same executives will look at quality and
relationships in the same way. One has to wonder what they
think is the real business of the executive. Thus the function
is always behind the rest of the company; and as an organization grows, it falls into predictable pits. Management does
not know how to ask for the information it needs; and when
a new requirement surfaces, finance has to scramble around
to make it happen.

A Journey through Financial
Purgatory—The Three Levels

The predictable financial pits can be separated into various
categories.

Companies with Revenues of Zero to 30 Million Dollars.
Companies of this size tend always to have cash-flow problems. They are not large enough to have a bank that loves them, so they must operate on a short-term line of credit which has to be brought to zero on a regular basis. Thus they must have relationships with their customers which keep the accounts receivables coming in on schedule. If they are in a business which requires the constant purchase of inventory, then they will always be working out deals with suppliers.

The financial systems for a company this size can usually keep up with what is going on because the number of transactions is not very large. However, customers will continually receive inaccurate invoices, which hinders rapid payment. This puts extra strain on the cash flow. If the company deals with intangibles, such as software, insurance, and such, they find themselves short of people due to reluctance of management to take on the burden of compensation. However, through a lot of hard work, scrambling, and manual calculation, they muddle along.

The Thirty-to-Sixty-Million-Dollar Image.   When this same company moves into the 30-to-60-million-dollar range, its financial system collapses. Suddenly, expenses that were not experienced before pop into the flow and margins begin to shrink. Many of these unknown expenses come from the company's expansion into other cities or countries or from the acquisition of another firm. Those who have never been through it just do not realize what it costs to open an office or store in another location. Doing it in a new country involves actions and costs that are beyond ordinary anticipation. Acquisitions are like setting up another household without letting the present one know about it. For a while, there are at least two of everything.

The financial system that took the company to this level of revenue now does not work properly. In the old days, a few key executives knew everything that was going on in the operation. They knew who was doing what. Now they find it difficult to even remember the names of all the employees.

The biggest problem companies of this size face in solving their financial management problems is the recognition that they need a stronger, more experienced, and thus more expensive, chief financial officer. Fifty million dollars revenue per year is the big time. Fortune 500 companies have several more zeros at the end of their numbers, but reporting and communicating requirements are very much the same. Also, it is not necessary to have a new office with dozens of people in order to experience unplanned costs. A tiny place with two people can make that happen, particularly if it is international.

Fifty Million Dollars and Up.   All other companies are encompassed within the 50-million-dollar end of range. Size brings the problem of communications, both internal and external. It is hard enough when everyone works in the same building, knows each other, and understands what the company does. When there are several divisions, thousands of employees who view the enterprise only through the narrow eyes of their departmental function, and several layers of management, then communication becomes a full-time job for the executive.

People lose their concept of the company as a whole and begin to think that everything revolves around their particular segment. The "togetherness" that senior executives talk about does not exist in the financial world when people are fighting for the same resources.

A Bird's Eye View of the Fundamentals of Finance

Anyone who reads this book probably has a working knowledge of financial management and might even get paid to run the financial operation in their organization. However, none of us is exempt from becoming one of those who tends to attract "black holes." It took a lot of thoughtful consideration, for instance, to refit the steel industry with obsolete technology some years ago. People who really understood money were the ones who turned the savings and loan business into a "black hole" of its own which threatens to suck in the entire United States government budget. Those firms that stuck to lending money on houses to people who were good risks are still in good shape. The others have created a magnetic field that will never be satisfied. This shows that none of us is secure in a protective bunker. Financial cockroaches can get in anywhere.

There has to be understanding on this, so an agreement must be reached on the definitions of the terms and systems involved. Here are a few of the important ones.

Accounts Payable. What we owe our suppliers for services rendered. It is necessary to have a clear policy on how fast we will pay and whether we pay it out of our revenues or borrow the money. If we have a good cash flow, we can take advantage of supplier discounts by paying quickly. Otherwise, we might want to hold off as long as possible. It is not good to be known as slow to pay. Others will think we do not have any money. Then again, the worst thing that can happen to a company is to run out of cash.

Accounts Receivable (ARs). What people owe us. Many companies provide a discount to customers who pay within 10 days or so. This discount is usually under 5 percent, but it adds up. Accounts receivable are usually tracked by the days it takes to collect them. Being paid within 30 days of sending out the bill is about as good as anyone does. Some companies get sloppy about this and have ARs that extend 90 and 120 days. Such accounts can lead to never getting paid. Since life goes on, most companies borrow money to keep operating while the customers are preparing to pay their bills. So a company that makes 10 percent pretax may be paying more than that to borrow. Feel the magnetic pull?

Budget. That document which categorizes, specifies, and controls company expenditures. I hate budgets and the budgeting process because I think that people should only spend what they need—and do that thriftily. In my large-corporation days budgets were hacked out with great concentration and reviewed continually. As a result, management always had a good, if after the fact, idea of where they were. Even so, they were continually surprised, which usually resulted in another monitoring point or function.

But I finally have to admit, after all these years, that people will not spend just the right amount for just the right things. People are revenue oriented and will always operate right at or beyond the amount of funds they see to be available in their crystal ball. They always think more will be forthcoming. That is the way they manage their personal accounts. The solution is always to get more money, not to reduce the outgo.

Expenses are the key to profitability. There is no revenue stream that cannot be outspent. Budgets lay out the limits that can be expended. Bells ring whenever these limits are approached or exceeded. At that time, the executive has to take action. It is not enough to hand out an assignment during the management meeting and require a report next month. The executive must become outraged that anyone could presume to threaten the very health of the company by exceeding allocations. The building needs to shake and rattle. The sinner must know that this is "*not* the way things are done around here."

Done properly, this will assure that the budgets are realistic and proper during the next period.

Cash Flow. A wonderful phrase that means pretty much what you want it to mean. Basically, it refers to the uncommitted cash received and available for use. It is somewhat like the so-called discretionary income for individuals. If we can pay our bills, meet our future needs, and stash something away for the future, then we have a cash flow worth measuring and talking about. However, outside of that, it is not of much use, except perhaps for putting a value on the organization.

Compensation. The salaries we pay our employees. It also includes the benefit programs. Benefits amount to at least 20 percent of salaries and in most companies go as high as 35 to 50 percent. These expenses are contained in health-care insurance, retirement programs, thrift plans, and such. The benefit programs are an important part of compensation and must be well thought out. They are hard to reduce or eliminate. If a company faces a temporary reduction in revenues, it is better to ask people to take a temporary pay reduction than to just lay off a bunch of them. No one ever trusts a company after a layoff.

Debt. A four-letter word that is not your friend. Long-term debt, such as mortgage on a property that will grow in value, is not too bad. The key is not to get into a situation where a dip in income would turn the property into a burden. When times are bad, it is very hard to sell things.

Dividends. Money paid out to shareholders from after-tax income. The battle is continually waged between those who want to use this money for reinvestment and those who want to distribute it. The key item is that dividends are not tax deductible for the company and the shareholder has to pay tax on it too. For this reason, governments like dividends to be paid. Strangely enough, corporations holding stock in other companies do not have to pay tax on dividends they get. Go figure.

Expenses. What gets paid out. They will rise of their own accord each year unless someone does something about it. People are added, services increased, research planned, projects commissioned, expansion plans implemented, and everything costs more than planned. It is here that the executive corps earns its money. It is hard to find a company that failed because its expenses were too low. Those who erased themselves through not using resources properly are legion. Executives must be consistent and keep their eyes on the purpose and policy of the corporation.

Most financial reporting concentrates on keeping track of

money received and spent. Just keeping neat records of over-spending is not money management.

Consider the financial overview of a health-care center (formerly known as a hospital). These organizations are in trouble financially because of the changes in the way things are paid for by the insurance companies and by the government. (People who were not sick pay the bills with some reluctance.)

- They are in trouble because of the cost of new technology.
- They are in trouble because of the popularity of malpractice suits.
- They are in trouble because of the need to treat those who have no way of repaying the service.
- They are in trouble because the medical professionals are going into competition with them on the profitable end of the business by establishing walk-in operations (called "Taco Doc" in the trade).

But mostly they are in trouble because these situations never really had to be managed before. The managers added up what things cost, added a profit, and sent out a bill (like AT&T before the breakup). Now, suddenly faced with a real and sometimes unfair life, they have to cope like the rest of us. If they could switch from concentrating on repairing people to helping people prevent disease, they would do well. That transformation might take some time. Right now, it is necessary to learn how to manage finances the way things are at this exact moment, and at the same time prepare for the future.

Gross Profit. The difference between revenues and expenses, also referred to as pretax income.

Line of Credit. A buffer of money to take care of the ups and downs in revenue. For this reason companies arrange a line of credit at a bank. This amount, usually equal to two or three months' revenues, should be drawn in as small amounts as possible and paid back quickly. Executives are tempted to use this readily available money for minicapital things. That is a very bad habit and will eventually put the company in the position of converting short-term debt to long-term. It is what I call the "black hole of Visa." Remember that no one ever gets into debt over his or her head on purpose. (I have started paying cash for restaurant meals rather than putting them on a card. This makes the servers happy but disturbs the owner and the IRS who lose track of tips.)

Net profit. Profit after all the expenses, including income taxes; also called after-tax income.

Revenues. Money received by the company from customers in return for services actually performed or products delivered. Revenues are what companies report that show up as "sales" in the financial press. Revenues are booked only when the product has been delivered or the service accomplished. Unless we deal in cash on delivery, the actual funds are not passed to us at the moment the exchange takes place; thus they are listed as accounts receivable.

Sales. Commitments made by customers to purchase whatever it is we provide.

Toward Eternal Financial Vigilance

Nothing comes easy in business. People seem not to want things to become easy. Everyone has a personal agenda. I have a story, which I stole from Bob Hope, about a couple who went to see a physician. The husband had not been feeling well. In fact, he was very depressed and not well at all. After a complete examination the doctor took the man to the waiting room and asked the wife to come into the office.

"Your husband is a very sick man," the doctor said. "He is going to need a lot of care."

"Whatever it takes, Doctor," she said. "We have a lot of money so that is no problem. I am a very successful attorney. I have cases in the Supreme Court and am consulted in Europe every month. We will do anything to get him well. There is nothing more important to me."

The doctor nodded. "There will be some expenses, but what your husband requires is personal attention. You will have to quit your job and stay home all the time. He needs three home-cooked meals each day, regular lovemaking, and constant reassurance."

The lady went back to the waiting room where the husband was. He looked up anxiously. "What did he say?" he asked.

The wife looked at him sadly. "He said you are going to die."

Financial integrity in an organization requires attention on a similar scale. Examination must be unrelenting because success, like liberty, requires eternal vigilance.

PART 2

Five Variations on the Theme of Becoming a Leader

5

A New Beginning

Explaining Executive Effectiveness—The Concept

In 41 years of corporate life Ed Kargston had faced many situations that offered ample opportunity for disruption. Disruption was not to his liking. Ed preferred life to be smooth and purposeful. He was for planned change on a constant basis, which meant that it would be useful and well thought out. He was recognized as a continual instigator of that system over the years because he felt that change could be produced without turmoil. Fertile fields could be created without volcanic eruptions. Marching in the streets was not his approach. He preferred a quiet hallway conversation with those who had the power. It was not necessary to be noisy in order to be effective.

His philosophy of the relationships which led to executive effectiveness had never been documented although he continually threatened to write a book about it. Everyone who worked with him for very long soon realized that he was deadly serious about what he called "I squared" (I^2). Information and implementation is what "I^2" meant. "Get the whole story and then do something about it," Ed would say.

"That doesn't sound very complicated, but if you look at

what keeps most people from getting things done, it's that they don't know what needs to happen. When they do take action, it is usually on the wrong thing or too late on the right thing—if they find it. I like to study the scene until I realize where the problem lies and decide what action to take. This doesn't take too long because most problems are not new. It is a lot better to spend time on preventing problems from happening at all."

Daydreaming

Ed's burly and somewhat paunchy figure was large enough to be intimidating. Yet he went out of his way to appear gentle and cooperative. He listened carefully, he took pains to be available to people, and he was genuinely a humble person. He was correctly known as a highly effective executive and had risen to become CEO in this very large and well-off organization. Having edged past 60 years of age, he was now spending more time thinking about leaving the company and becoming involved in some later-life career. He had been offered several opportunities to join business schools as a professor but was reluctant to become involved in official academic life. It seemed to be restrictive. "Have to show up for class every day," he mused. Somehow that smacked of regimentation.

So as he proceeded across the parking lot at the end of the work day, he was automatically retracing the thought process he had revisited before: what to do after retirement—what to really do. He did not want to do just busy work and he intended to resign from the Board of Directors of the company. Tommie would be surprised about that, but hanging on in that way would not be useful. It would be impossible not to become involved in the affairs of the company and, after all these years, the younger folks should be given their own chances to have some fun.

Being an executive *was* fun. At least he had always looked at it that way. That time in the bread plant when the manager had said that it was not possible to reduce waste to a lower level, for instance. Ed had found a worker who had an idea about making a dramatic reduction in damaged product. It seemed that a pig farmer came every couple of days to the plant and hauled away a large truckload of broken and damaged product. Most of this waste was the result of packages falling from the assembly line or being damaged during routine material handling.

The worker had told Ed during his walk around the plant that guard rails in certain spots would protect the products as they moved along. Ed had encouraged the industrial engineer to alter the line process and had personally promoted the worker when it was all over. The general manager had been reconditioned and transformed into a more open-minded person. He was the one who suggested the prize-winning slogan the employees hung up to remind themselves that such waste would ultimately cost them the plant. *If you drop it, you eat it,* said the sign. Everyone was happy except the pig farmer. There was not enough waste to make the trip worthwhile to him anymore.

Or how about years ago when the old man wanted to start a finance business and everyone was against it? Ed had been able to make the operation happen, and today that unit produces 30 percent of the corporation's profit. It was much more profitable to lend out the cash flow at 18 percent interest than put it in bonds paying less than half that much.

To participate in those kinds of experiences on a daily basis required a place for them to happen and enough people to be involved on every side of the question. There had to be offices, plants, unions, customers, banks, competition—the complete cast of characters. He had a good imagination, but fantasy would never take the place of real life. It was clear to him that Ellen was not going to let him reorganize their personal life very much. She had very firm ideas about his future role and was insistent that he come up with a couple of genuine outside interests before staying home for good. She had no intention of giving up her interesting life to sit around and listen to him spin tales about the good old days.

They both had attended a recent dinner for a friend who had been retired for six months. After being roasted, the honoree talked about some of the fascinating things he had been doing at home. All of the canned goods were now stacked in alphabetical order, the forks all pointed the same way in the silver drawers, and the daily mail was delivered to each member of the household on time.

It was not that Ed had no interests; there were dozens of things that involved him. He was even now very active in public service, serving on commissions that the mayor and the governor had established. He was on the boards of three charitable operations and had been instrumental in working out the scheme that put the symphony back in good financial shape. He never went to the concerts because he didn't care for the music. Ellen seemed to understand this, but others had trouble with it. Was it unreasonable to work on something worthwhile without participating in its actual performance? He didn't care to watch little-league baseball either, but he contributed to its survival.

The children were doing well on their own. His grandchildren took up some of his time, although now that they were halfway across the country, he didn't get to see them as much as he wanted.

"That would be a good project for the future," he thought. "Perhaps we could rent one of those motor homes and go visiting six or seven times a year?"

He had seen dozens of the RV units when he and Ellen drove up to Canada one summer to take a vacation north of Lake Louise. As they toured Banff and the national park, he became deeply involved with the landscape—the massive mountains, the glaciers, the river turned green by glacier dust. The campers seemed so carefree as they parked alongside the streams that it appeared to be an attractive lifestyle. However, each evening when it came time to quiet down and he was interested in a hot bath, a cup of coffee, and a good meal, he remembered that hotels had a lot of charm and convenient facilities even if they were more expensive.

Money was not going to be a problem. He had always been
well compensated and there were few expenses. They would
be able to travel comfortably, but he had spent half of his life
traveling, so what kind of deal was that? Bouncing around
Europe with 38 other seniors on a tour bus was not going to
be his future. That much he knew. Besides there were not
many places left to see.

Ed was becoming irritated with himself again as he drove.
It was just too late to wait until retirement was staring a person right in the eye to work out a plan. He had known this
for years and yet had never done anything about it. It was
like having heart disease and pretending it was not really
there. He had never faced this sort of indecision during his
career. His normal practice of gathering information and
then deciding would not work all by itself. There had to be
an acceptance on his part that he wanted to solve or prevent
something if information were to be projected or absorbed.
It was very hard to gather information when the primary
data source, himself, was uncooperative.

Back to Reality: On the Links
with the "Nine-Hole League"

As Ed arrived at the municipal golf course, other members of
the "nine-hole league" were in various stages of preparation.
Men and women from all over the company participated in
the league each Thursday evening during the summer. Ed
never missed when he was in town. Besides enjoying the golf,
he found it a wonderful opportunity to keep in touch with
what he called the "real people" of the organization. Joining
only required an interest in golf and the expenditure of $7
each outing. Two dollars of that went toward the annual dinner and awards. The rest was for greens fees since everyone
pulled their own golf carts or carried bags.

He had changed clothes in his office, so he scrambled to
switch shoes, take the clubs out of the car trunk, and get to

the first tee. In the process he was greeted by Harriet Swenson, one of the purchasing supervisors.

"We're playing together tonight," she said. "Carl Smith and Walt Levine are the rest of our foursome. We're next on the tee."

"Great, Harriet," Ed replied. "How have you been hitting them?"

As they chatted and walked toward the tee, Ed realized once again that most of his fellow golfers didn't call him anything. He had encouraged them to call him "Ed," but few did. They seemed to know that he was not comfortable with "Mr. Kargston." Since he was the only senior member of management who belonged to the golf league, they all just went along with the status as it was.

Tommie, the chairman, played in the tennis league and everyone called him Mr. Thompson. "Great shot, Mr. Thompson," seemed okay for Tommie. In fact, the only time Ed's first name was used was when someone said something like "Great shot, Ed." Perhaps the reason it was not a more frequent occurrence had more to do with his game than his title.

At any rate, they all greeted each other. The men drove first. Then the group walked up to the red tees for Harriet's drive. She hit it several yards past two of the other balls and there was a good deal of comment about "woman's rights" and the advantages of having different tees. Harriet assured them that she would be glad to play them even on a course that a woman had designed.

"There is no reason for holes to be so long," she said. "Only the professionals need 400 yards to make it tough. Most of us need three shots to get to the green from that distance. I would get rid of the long holes and play everything 300 yards or under."

She looked at Ed and nodded, "What do you think of that strategy?"

Ed sighed.

"My experience," he noted, "is that I seem to score the

same on every course regardless of whether it is hard or easy. I just find different ways of failing. The real part of the game is around the green. If you can chip and putt, everything else takes care of itself."

"You sure have a way of getting right at the heart of things," said Carl. "We like to pretend that we could change the golf courses to make it easier for us. You go right to the one thing that would make a big change, and it is also the one thing we never spend any time working on. We all know it, but we don't do it. Why is that?"

"Beats me," said Ed. "Most times people know what's good for them, but they refrain from doing it. Or they do something that they know is not good for them."

"Like smoking," said Harriet, lighting a cigarette.

"Or gobbling too many calories," said Carl, as he opened a candy bar.

Ed smiled. "I do notice that people change their habits when they understand more about the effect of what they are doing. I gave up caffeine, for instance, when I realized that it was contributing to my nervousness. However, I have not convinced myself that a couple of hours a week on the practice green would be better for my golf health."

As the group approached the second green, the sky suddenly erupted with thunder and the beginnings of a rain shower. They all moved rapidly toward a nearby shelter. Just as they arrived, the rain began in earnest.

"This doesn't look too serious," said one of the golfers. "I suspect it will be over in about 10 minutes."

They all sat in silence for a while. Times such as this seem to be designed for a little quiet reflection, thought Ed. There are no requirements or opportunities for doing anything; it is not necessary to feel guilty about the lack of activity; the atmosphere is pleasant; the company is fine. It was a good time for idle chatter and daydreaming.

"Are you going to retire?" asked Carl.

"Huh?" said Ed.

"I didn't mean to be forward, but the guys have been wondering. We would all hate to see you leave the company. You're easy to talk to."

They all glanced nervously at Carl and then at Ed, who had regained his composure enough to smile.

"Well, I guess we all have to do it one day, Carl. I've been thinking about it. Actually, I have a little while to go before they clean out my desk."

"You could keep on playing in the league, couldn't you?" asked Walt. "If there is some rule against it, you might get it changed before the time comes."

"What are you going to do when you retire?" asked Harriet.

"Don't worry about that, Harry," smiled Walt. "I'll bet he's got something all lined up. Isn't that right?"

Ed was beginning to wonder about this, but if you're going to be part of the group, then you'd better be part of the group. He just chatted away like the rest of them.

"Actually I've been giving it some thought, but I have come to no conclusions. In fact, I would welcome suggestions. We can agree right now that I probably would not be a golf professional. I've never been anything but a manager of one kind or another. What do you think I should do?"

The group looked a little bewildered for a moment and then began to consider the matter as a serious assignment.

"I thought people in your kind of situation just got on the boards of a lot of companies and continued active involvement as long as they wanted to," said Harriet.

"That can be true," nodded Ed. "But I've always been more active than that permits. Boards are all right; but as long as the CEO is performing well, there's very little for a board to do. It does let you keep in touch with people though."

"How about teaching? Couldn't you train people to be executives? There sure aren't very many of them. There are a lot of managers, and some darn good ones, but not many executives," said Carl.

"Yeah," said Walt. "I remember that you talked once about

the difference between managers and executives. You'd be good at that. Have you thought about teaching?"

"I've been asked to work with a couple of colleges, but somehow that doesn't seem the right thing. Most of the guidance I've given over the years has been to people who are already working at some level in a company. For instance, if you'll recall, that talk of the difference between executives and managers was part of an after-hours company program on general management. Everyone there already had a common vocabulary of business. Talking to college students would be a whole different bag."

"Well, how about doing it for those who might become executives someday?" asked Harriet.

"I'm not certain I follow you, Harriet," said Ed.

She jumped up and moved to the side of the hut, waving her finger in the air.

"I mean working with those who have already shown that they're on the way up or have the potential to get there. You could help a few of those people who might have a big effect on what goes on in the world."

"Yeah," said Walt. "Why waste time on those who are never going to amount to anything?"

"But how do you know who is going to be a useful achiever and who is going to make a lot of purposeless trouble?" asked Ed. "I've always had a hard time picking and choosing. A lot has to do with the willingness to work, but most of being an executive comes down to attitude and smarts."

"You could give them IQ tests," said Walt.

Ed shook his head.

"That isn't the kind of smart I mean. My experience has been that highly intelligent people can be good executives but usually are not. They seem to lack patience with the rest of us. However, if they're smart, they can learn, I guess. IQ tests would be helpful, but then coping with life is a test that is real."

Harriet was beginning to hope the rain would keep up.

"If you had a class of people with good potential, what

would they need to learn? I mean in broad terms. Suppose they already knew about balance sheets and stuff like that. What are the things an executive needs to learn to do?"

Ed began to think that while this was becoming a bit involved, it was helping him sort the situation out. Perhaps his fellow golfers were unwittingly showing him the way.

"Well, just off the top of my cap, I would think they need to learn something about setting policy on the right things: finance, quality, and relationships. There's a lot more involved than just knowledge and intensity. They would have to learn how to create the right work environment and do it on purpose. Those are the key things to being successful, along with personal intensity and attitude."

"I suspect you've been thinking about this," said Harriet.

"Perhaps without realizing it," nodded Ed. "Well, it looks like the rain is gone, and the folks behind us are teeing up. I want to thank all of you for helping my retirement plans."

"It is purely selfish, Ed," said Carl. "We would like to see the world get some good executives."

Resolve

As the idea began to blossom in Ed's mind over the next few weeks, his golf game went even further downhill. It was hard to concentrate when so many plans and thoughts were bubbling around in his head. Since a golf swing took a couple of seconds at most, it became apparent that he had to work all this out before anything was going to change.

If he could work with a few people, those who had the capability, it might be possible to add to their expectancy of success and do it in a reasonable period of time. Six months of "tutoring" would be about right. They would have to come on their own with their corporation providing support and paying an unreasonable fee. They would also continue to work. That practice would keep them involved in the real world. Instead of case histories based on the past, they would deal with what was happening all around them. He would bring them together for discussion sessions and spend individual time with each one.

The idea would be to accelerate their learning process so they would not have to spend 40 years and be approaching retirement before they really knew how to be executives. Obviously, they would have to be willing to learn and to work. He would take three at first.

It was time to make a few calls.

6

Organizing Kargston Associates

Every dream collides with reality sooner or later. In Ed's case this took the form of realizing that the first thing he was going to require for this venture would be customers who would supply both students and revenues. This would be no problem if he could identify people who were genuinely interested in the need for executive development. For this reason he decided to have a friendly lunch.

Tommie Thompson, chairman of Ed's company, Estate, insisted on hosting the meeting after Ed laid out his idea. The company had a policy of retiring executives at age 60 and although the Board had offered to make an exception in Ed's case for a year or two, he felt this would just be postponing the inevitable. He did agree to stay on the Board for two more years after separation.

Tommie had always supported personnel development programs put forth by the human resources operations. But in his heart he felt that those who were going to develop did so on their own and that the conventional approaches to creating executives offered little hope. Tommie was fond of stating that he learned very little in college due to his own lack of concentration and had been forced to educate himself. Since Estate had grown by a factor of three during Tommie's years there, it would appear that he had done a good job of learning.

Tommie was interested in Ed's idea because he had found that the biggest obstacle to enlarging the corporation worldwide was the short supply of people who could get things done right. He believed that an executive corps equipped with the right discipline and knowledge could conquer the entire business community. He had wanted Ed to just concentrate on Estate, but Ed did not want to limit his work to one company because he wanted to establish a teaching organization that could be effective for a long time. If he could determine how to set up a transferable system of executive creation, that would be quite an accomplishment. The guests began to arrive for the luncheon.

Betty Forrest, CEO of Alabank, was a "twenty-first-century woman" according to a recent *Time* magazine cover story. She was embarrassed by the attention she received as a female executive, insisting that a person's sex made no difference to the bottom line of a financial statement. Her tough-minded way of operating had made her an unofficial member of the White House Economic Council. And through the programs she had instituted, her bank was recognized as the innovator in information management. She had worked for Ed 20 years ago as an intern and always made certain that she credited him for his part in helping her have a successful career.

Betty had created an informal communication system of female executives across the country in an effort to build an "old-girl network." The network had been very useful in helping women to learn about opportunities, but to date it had not had much effect on moving women past that invisible but very real senior-executive barrier. Until some of the "old girls" reached the very top of their pyramid, they could not help each other over the wall. She was interested in learning how to teach "wall vaulting" to the talented and intense young women who were impatiently circling while trying to break through.

Wallace Smith, CEO of Eastland, was not one who attended meetings outside his office. He was making an exception today under protest, only because Tommie would not accept a negative answer. Wallace had expressed concern to Tommie at one time about the way young people were trained to become leaders, and Tommie reminded him of it. Wallace, who was 76 years old, controlled what had been a family business. He still treated it that way, which was not well received in the financial community.

The question he heard most often was one of succession. The older man had appointed several executives as his next-in-line but always found them lacking after a year or two. They would be dismissed and go on to a bigger and better job where they usually were not very successful. This proved his point about their competence but raised even more questions about his ability to select an heir. He came to this meeting with the forlorn hope that whatever it was about could produce a Mr. or Ms. Right for him. In his heart he knew that no one could ever handle his job properly.

Jim Andling, CEO of Marlot, was a man on the go. He had taken over the widespread corporation three years ago and as his first act listed all the operations that were making money on one sheet of paper and those that were not doing well on another. He gave one sheet to Alex Bennett with instructions to manage the winners, and the other sheet to Lex Gorberg with instructions to sell the losers. Then he sat down with the director of administration and did the same thing with the list of corporate executives. He was generous and discreet with the ones who were asked to leave; but leave they did, the very next day.

Streamlining complete, Andling used the resulting cash to stalk companies that would fit into his concept. He had accomplished several hostile takeovers of companies, released their senior management immediately, trimmed expenses dramatically, and turned them into much more profitable operations. In most cases he was able to promote younger executives to run these companies. However, being inexperienced, they required a lot of direction, which forced him to spend a great deal of time in meetings and travel. He dreamed of finding a system or operation that would produce the executives he needed, thus his agreement to come to the luncheon.

He had begun an effort inside Marlot. The management development people had set up a school that all upcoming managers and executives attended. Jim made a point of visiting each class to let them know personally how important they were to the future, and present, of the corporation. The result was a high level of communication and confidence within Marlot, but he was concerned with the absence of obviously outstanding young people. He also was becoming a little nervous about the turnover rate at senior levels.

Testing the Waters

After everyone had ordered lunch, Ed felt it was time to begin. At the first moment of silence he spoke up, thanking them for coming, and launched into the purpose of the meeting.

"All of us would like to find someone who does the right thing at the right time for the right reason. We would like to be able to hand something over with absolute confidence that understandable goals would be laid out, that the task, whatever it was, would be accomplished smoothly, and that we would have successes and no troubles. We would like to find people who can innovate and implement, all in the same package. Is that correct?" asked Ed.

"In a nutshell," said Andling. "I'd like to find a constant supply of people like that—people who can continue to grow and still keep their perspective."

"Can these people be mass produced, Ed?" asked Betty.

"Are you going to set up a factory for them?" She smiled at the thought.

"We'd have to gather them up at six months of age, Betty," replied Ed. "I think I don't have 35 years to invest in that approach."

Wallace Smith had been staring at Ed since he sat down. It was apparent that he was not sure this was something that would fit his plans.

"How are you going to go about this executive growing, Mr. Kargston?" he asked. "How long does it take to produce them, and how many can you do a year?"

Pressing the Advantage

Ed nodded and turned to look directly at Smith.

"I am going to go about it as much one-on-one as possible, Mr. Smith. My thought is to take individuals you have identified as showing obvious signs of potential, provided they look that way to me, too. They would have to be very bright, smart rather than intellectual; they would need ambition and energy; and they would have to be willing to learn.

"As for output, I would think that it will take about six months from the time they accept me for them to be headed on the right path. That time would be very intensive. They would continue in their jobs, and we would talk about what they were doing on a continuous basis. We would have some workshops with all the students during the period."

"Why did you say 'from the time they accept me'?" asked Betty. "Don't you assume they will come into the program with a positive approach? You have a national reputation as an executive; I would think they would be very eager to hop right in and get started."

"One would think so," said Ed, "but my experience has been that this kind of person needs to be convinced personally that such an effort would be good for them. Many colleges have executive MBA programs, for instance, where people who have been out of school and working for several years can attend one full day a week for two years and get an MBA degree. It is very concentrated but effective. My friends in that work say they always have to spend the first few weeks helping each class become convinced that there just might be something about management they do not already know."

"Would you be close enough to the details of the corporations to help them with their problems, Ed?" asked Jim. "It seems it would take you a lot of time to come up to speed. I spend all day doing that at Marlot, and I still get lost every now and then."

"Ed never worries about what's going on," said Tommie. "He can find out more about everything quicker than anyone I ever saw. People spill their deepest secrets to him."

"We won't be spending much time on the details of company operations, Jim," replied Ed. "I've always thought that the work of an executive revolves around three areas: finance, quality, and relationships. If we can learn to handle those, everything else takes care of itself. The environment of the corporation is formed, everyone knows what they are doing, and the right actions take place."

"That sounds like a bunch of slogans, Mr. Kargston," said Wallace Smith. "What do you mean about the 'environment' of the organization?"

Ed waved his hand to take in the ambience of the club room where they were sitting.

"It's easy to see the environment here, for instance. The club has been set up so the members and their guests can be comfortable. Everything is understated. The staff is practically invisible. They come and go and you never notice. When people come in for a meal or a drink, they automatically speak softly and pleasantly, and the whole atmosphere is very positive. The management of the club causes all this to happen because they have determined what the membership wants. They spend a lot of time behind the scenes training the staff to anticipate, and be quiet about it; selecting menus; and working each detail.

"In a company management creates the atmosphere by the way they act and direct. Some companies are pleasant places to work, some are chaotic. The point is that it can all be done on purpose. A great part of the success of the operation depends on the managerial environment. In most places it is all done by accident."

Smith was interested in this.

"So you would teach them to arrange things in a certain and very specific way?"

Ed shook his head.

"Not necessarily. I would be more concerned that they begin to realize that this is something they have to face up to and cause to happen properly. There is no standard company environment that fits all. But every executive creates one whether he or she plans to or not, and it has a very real effect on what happens."

"What else does an executive have to make happen?" asked Betty.

"Well," said Ed, "they need a constancy of purpose if they are going to do something that lasts. If they are involved only in survival, for instance, nothing they do will be around for very long. They need to establish relationships with their people, with customers, with the government, with everybody.

"When I say finance, quality, and relationships, I'm talking about the core of executive work. The most effective leaders in history have understood that."

"Who were some of the people you consider to be great leaders of history, Ed?" asked Tommie. "Who do you set up as examples?"

"Be careful, Ed," said Wallace Smith. "I've been around for a long time. I know most of the historical characters."

Everyone laughed.

"Well, I won't go back too far, Wallace," said Ed. "But it's an interesting thought. Let me just rattle off the names of a few well-known leaders and give you my opinion of their effectiveness.

"Abraham Lincoln came into office at the worst possible time for the nation and for himself. He was not popular, the nation was completely unprepared for the situation, and even his cabinet felt he was incompetent.

"He stated that his job was to bring the Union back together, and he never wavered from that one policy for the next four and a half years. He selected executives who were willing to accept that goal and he supported them. No matter what happened he kept that in front of him every day.

"He said something like: 'If freeing all the slaves would save the Union, I would do that; if freeing none would save the Union, I would do that; if freeing some and doing nothing about the others would save the Union, I would be willing to do that also.'

"By his leadership he was able to convince everyone that they had better concentrate on the most important job. And the results of his work are with us today. He is appreciated now as he was not then. Everyone who goes to Washington visits his statue.

"Many famous leaders are not appreciated because their goals were for personal achievement only. People like Stalin and Napoleon, for instance, left less lasting footprints. Similarly, by now, most of Stalin's statues have been torn down. Napoleon set up a complex system that only he could operate. When he was thought to have been killed during the retreat from Moscow, it never occurred to anyone to declare his son, the King of Rome, as Emperor. Napoleon was very upset when he got to Paris.

"Eisenhower was a masterful executive. He brought together all kinds of impossible people to overcome impossible obstacles. He was able to keep them concentrating on the target and at the same time did not give up any of the responsibilities he held personally. He was a master at relationships.

"Churchill was a great strategist and communicator. He didn't do much about relationships, but people would die for him anyway. If he hadn't been where he was when he was, the world would be a much different place now. Churchill was probably the only indispensable person involved in World War II.

"Jesus of Nazareth was a witnessing executive. He never wrote any memos or even set up an organization, but He laid out principles and concepts that are still growing. He had more effect on the world than anyone else."

Over the Top

Jim was ready to start some action concerning Ed's project.

"What exactly do you want us to do, Ed? I think what you're getting into here could be very valuable to our operation and, I think, to all of us. How would you set it up?"

"I've written a brief memo covering it and will give all of you a copy before we break up. But basically, I was thinking that each of you would nominate one or two individuals. I would meet with them; and if everything was agreeable, we would put together the first class. We would plan on a six-month relationship at first.

"The class and I would work out our own schedule and system. I'm sure that will become much more structured as we learn how to do this thing. As time goes on and you determine if you are satisfied with the results, we will put together other classes. I think that over a three-year period I could handle six or seven individuals from each of you.

"By that time I hope to have established a system that will make executive development less dependent on my personal participation. I'm not certain at this time how it is going to come about, but I do have some ideas on the subject.

"So if you're interested, please select the participants, ask them to give me a call, and we'll go from there. I've moved out of Estate and set up a small place of my own. So far, the name is Kargston Associates, Inc. The invoices for the program are in the envelope. If you want to participate, just sign one and send it along to your finance department. You will never get another bill, at least not for this group. I think it's easier to set one fee. We'll take care of everything out of that."

Ed paused and looked around the table.

Wallace Smith reached in his jacket pocket and removed an envelope which he handed to Ed.

"Here are two names and résumés. These are the people I would like to include in your course. One is not so young and one is not so old. You tell me after a few months which one I should make president and my successor. I promise you that I will let that person take over the job if you think he or she is capable."

Everyone looked at Smith in amazement.

"That is quite a vote of confidence," said Tommie. "I think it's a fascinating idea."

"I'm honored, Wallace," said Ed. "I'll keep in close touch with you on this. I assume the individuals named in the envelope do not know about this."

"You can be certain they don't," said Wallace. "I have enough trouble with people wanting to take my temperature and feel my pulse every day as it is. I'm sure there must be a pool on for when I'm going to that great board room in the sky."

"Well, I'm not quite ready to anoint anyone," said Jim Andling, "but I'm anxious to participate. I'll have two names for you this afternoon, Ed."

"Me too," said Betty. "You can assume that they will be women."

"One of mine is of that persuasion," said Wallace, "and I suspect that several of Ed's flock will qualify. I know you think we're all trying to exclude females, Betty, but it just isn't true. Some of my best friends are women."

Betty laughed and patted his wrist.

"I know, I know. Your company has been very open. We haven't done as well with Marlot or even with Estate, as we have with you. But there is progress all along the line."

"Is that right?" asked Andling. "I see a lot of women managers around. I thought we were doing better."

"Take a look at who's in the important meetings, Jim. That's where the good jobs are. But you're doing better. The Marlot personnel department had a bad reputation among all minorities, but lately I'm hearing that they are much more openly aggressive in reaching out."

"We have a new director," said Jim. "We found him after a long search. When he came to interview me, he started by saying 'You might have noticed that I'm black, but what you don't know is that I'm married to a Hispanic woman. We can almost solve your minority problem by ourselves.' He has done a great deal to change attitudes around there.

"His assistant is a very bright young lady, and I was thinking of nominating her for Ed's class. The other person I was thinking about runs one of our plants in Ohio. But I'm not sure he's ever been to college. Do you think Ed would have a problem with that?"

Betty shook her head.

"I think Ed doesn't care where they come from as long as they have the basics and the desire. But you might ask him."

Second Thoughts

As they all left together, Ed began to feel concern about how all this was going to come together. It was one thing to conceive something. It was quite another to pull it off. He was going to have to make certain that the individuals he selected to participate had the potential to be even more successful than they anticipated. No one ever knows his or her own true worth; no one ever knows in advance what he or she could accomplish.

Ed himself could remember a time when he would have signed up for a lifetime career as a department head. At one time that role seemed out of reach. So he could not hang out a sign and say, "Come to Ed's shop. We will make you a CEO or your money back." Actually, it was not their money anyway; and, come to think of it, they were not even participating on their own initiative.

That might be a problem. If people looked at this as some sort of routine, corporate charm school, they might not give it their best effort. He would have to imagine how he would have dealt with Lincoln, Eisenhower, or Churchill if they had appeared at his door as young, upcoming executives. It was pretty unsettling to think of dealing with folks like that.

He knew that they were learners and that they constantly were searching for more information. But it was difficult to imagine them sitting in a circle at his feet as he philosophized on the vagaries of asset management. People of that capacity select their own teachers.

But then George Marshall and Franklin Roosevelt (FDR) were two people who knew talent when they saw it. They both had lists they had gathered over the years of individuals who had the talent and content to be leaders. That's how Eisenhower went from major to two-star general in only two years. Those lists produced the people who ran the nation's war effort.

But FDR and Marshall were able to offer people command; they were actually in charge of the operation. In this situation there was nothing to offer directly except information obtained from experience and thought. The person would have to be thirsting for it. It couldn't just be thrust upon them. He was going to determine exactly how to approach those who would become his students. He was going to have to create and then implement this system.

But, after all, that's what being an executive is all about.

7

The Participants

Ed believed in doing homework—not enough to create boredom, but something that would let him know what was happening. He had asked for résumés of those who were recommended for participation in the program and had received those plus the comments of their respective CEOs and a personality analysis supplied by each personnel department. He had no idea that such evaluations were routine at that level. His own company, Estate, even did it (which made him decide to go down and take a look at his own file one of these days).

Taking this information, he prepared a summary sheet for his own reference. Ed was not one to let others make up his mind about the worthiness of individuals, but it was important to know how these folks came across to others. Often this interaction was what kept success on the back burner. We rarely see ourselves as others do, an idea set to poetry by Robert Burns some time ago and still true now. If we could only sit and watch ourselves in action, we might be able to correct all those inadequacies.

Or would we? Ed remembered an experiment conducted by a clinic specializing in alcoholics. They videotaped a couple of alcoholics while they were in full swing, performing at their disgusting best. The next day the offenders were shown the tapes only to sit there unmoved. They just did not relate the film to themselves. They didn't recognize the "actors" as the persons they knew best. Seeing the actions that others complained about had no effect. He supposed it was like trying to convince snorers that they snore. When they're awake, nothing is going on.

Nick Winston, 40. Marlot.   President of Electronic Division, youngest division president, previously corporate purchasing director. College in Midwest, football player—an academic all-American. Golfer, skier, walker. Keeps self fit. Does not smoke, drinks casually.

> FAMILY: Wife, Marilyn (met in college), and two teenage children.
>
> PERSONALITY: Impatient but good with people. Detached. Smooth and thoughtful. Effective in getting results. Reads on planes and when possible at home. Considers himself well-read. Tough-minded. Respects authority.
>
> CEO COMMENTS: Nick is moving up fast because he has earned it and because he could go elsewhere anytime he wanted to. He is well-liked by his peers and has really turned the Electronics Division around in a few months. Morale is the highest it has ever been and former customers are giving us another chance.
>
> KARGSTON NOTES: I have seen Nick in action. He is effective in comfortable situations but has difficulty with the unusual. Occasionally immature in actions. However, he is made of the right stuff if anyone is.
>
> CONCLUSION: Unless something shows up in personal interview, invite him to join the group.

Elizabeth Commons, 38. Eastland.   Law degree, but did not care for it and now is corporate marketing director. Being prepared to head the strategy and planning operation.

FAMILY: Husband, Charles, is a research scientist. They have two children and pride themselves on sharing the parenting job. They do charity work together, concentrating mostly on teenagers who are having a hard time. Neither Charles nor Elizabeth suffered privation or abuse during childhood.

PERSONALITY: Attractive woman with confidence in herself. Well educated and informed, she is pleasant to others at all times yet firm in her demands and expectations. Not particularly people oriented but is considered charming.

SPORTS: Likes tennis but dislikes clubs.

CEO COMMENTS: Elizabeth is one of the two I am considering to be president of the company. She is extremely bright and learns quickly. I think a couple of years in strategy and planning will give her the understanding she needs. She is very eager to achieve.

KARGSTON NOTES: Elizabeth has a great deal of talent and smarts. Would like to have her in this program. Somehow women grow up in business without being permitted to really know what is going on. I mean this in the sense that a woman could be a fine announcer of a football game, but she will never know what it is like to play it. Men have the same situation with babies. We would have to see how hard she is willing to work.

Harold Clark, 55. Eastland. General manager of Finance Company. Started the operation from scratch and without the support of top management. Very forceful person without a great deal of personal charm. Speaks up to Wallace Smith when others do not. Attended accounting college but did not graduate. Went to work to support mother and sister.

FAMILY: Wife, Mildred, and three sons in college. Mother and sister still being supported in another town.

PERSONALITY: Positive but rather bland. Will sit quietly unless drawn in.

CEO COMMENTS: Harold is a very dependable, strong person who builds solid organizations. He has his own ideas on things but is willing to listen. His division is the most profitable one we have. He is my other CEO candidate.

KARGSTON NOTES: Harold is deeper than he appears.

Anna Novello, 32. Alabank. Anna has been through several building jobs in the bank, her current one being branch manager in a new suburban unit outside Birmingham. Very active in civic affairs, is vice president of Chamber of Commerce. People are shocked when they realize how sharp she is. Belongs to drama group.

FAMILY: Unmarried but dates one person regularly.

PERSONALITY: Outgoing and pleasant. A little defensive about doing so well at such a young age. Wants to make certain people do not give being female and Hispanic some of the credit.

CEO COMMENTS: Anna is young, but she will outgrow that. Her employees work harder for her than any manager we have, and she is relentless about getting new business for the bank. Good future.

KARGSTON NOTES: She is more mature than I expected.

Alvin Austin, 36. Estate Corp. Corporate purchasing manager. (Number two job in that function corporate-wide.) Earnest and dedicated. Represents a new breed in purchasing, very much into long-range arrangements with suppliers rather than just low price. The Estate vice president of purchasing will be retiring in two years, and Alvin is being prepared to take his place.

FAMILY: Married three years ago. Wife, Alice, was a widow with two young children. Alvin has adopted them. He and Alice have a one-year-old girl. Alvin has no outside interests besides his work and his family. Considers himself a "nerd," proudly.

PERSONALITY: Very bright and alert. Pleasant, but firm underneath.

CEO COMMENTS: Alvin is a comer. He is narrowly focused at present, concentrating primarily on purchasing.

KARGSTON NOTES: Not sure about Alvin, but we'll see.

Probing Executive Attitudes

Each individual had been asked to provide a self-rating according to the characteristics required of an executive. Ed did not like scales, so he limited the response to plus or minus, plus being an asset and minus being something that needed work. The purpose of this was to let him see how well they knew themselves. Very bright people tended to manipulate evaluations like this in order to control the tester. That is why they did well on tests: they were smarter than the ones who had prepared them. As a result, it was not always possible to apply such measures to people like this, or at least to believe the results.

However, he felt that after a while he would know them well enough to recognize what characteristics and attitudes they possessed. That was what made the difference in the success levels of smart people. He had known dozens who should have made it big but failed to get over the first couple of ditches. Attitudes about themselves and the world seemed to be the main deterrent. A lot of people condemn themselves to predetermined lifestyles through the attitudes they select. This is true in every area, not just with the executives we are trying to raise.

For instance, some people consider themselves "sick." This is different from having an illness, which is something that is expected to go away after treatment or a certain amount of time. Sick people *always* have something wrong; they continually seek medical assistance and usually quarrel with their doctors. Sickness becomes the ruling factor in their lives. In personal economics it is the difference between being "poor" and "broke." Poor is the knowledge that we will never have enough money to live on; broke is being short of funds but knowing that it can be fixed with a little effort. Poor becomes a lifestyle and is as self-fulfilling as being sick. Broke and ill are temporary and do not interfere with a person's management of his or her life.

Executives who feel they don't receive enough appreciation condemn themselves to career unhappiness because there never are enough thank yous to go around. Even those who have reached the CEO level, who are sought out for national honorary committees, who are invited to whisper in the ears of the politically mighty, can suffer from this condition. They are "poor and sick" while sitting on a throne surrounded by adoring underlings. If they were to receive the Nobel Prize for management (which would be a first), they would be concerned that the king spent more time with other recipients or that the recognition was very long overdue.

Other executive attitude problems revolve around the insistence on short-term results which will let them move up the ranks quicker. Then there are those who cannot trust anyone to do a job completely. If they run into someone who does a proper job, they keep changing the requirements to make it come out their way. The oblivious executive is so concentrated on a private agenda that others do not enter into the equation at all. This is the "Mr. McGoo style" of management; the hero bumbles along with no real idea of what is happening, yet somehow others see him as able to produce.

Ed picked up the list of "minus" ratings done by the group and reviewed it.

- Nick: Sensitive, humble
- Elizabeth: Learner, reliable, sensitive, humble
- Harold: Sensitive, intense, pleasant
- Anna: Humble
- Alvin: Learner, available, energetic

Ed decided that Anna's rating of herself as "needs work" in being humble was made clear by her not needing work in all the other areas. After all, how can you be humble if you think everything else is in good shape? Liz and Alvin both admitted to putting too little effort into learning. The others had that problem also but did not recognize, or admit, it. Well, at least he had the beginnings of an understanding.

The most significant problem in executive life was ego—ego both ways: too much and not enough. If our opinion of ourselves was beyond reality in either direction, then failure was inevitable. A person could feel infallible or without merit. Obviously, somewhere between would reflect a proper balance. It was a puzzlement that was probably not going to be solved by this exercise, but one that remained at the center of directing any organization.

The Final Cut

The individual interviews all went well, and Ed selected enough people for a second class to begin after the first one was over. Nick, Elizabeth, Harold, Anna, and Alvin formed the first group and agreed that they would have at least one session together. After that, they were hoping that Ed would become personally involved with the development of each in a one-on-one setting. They felt he would be able to see the way they were working and then help them adjust their approach. They all were delighted with the opportunity presented by this arrangement; but, at the same time, they felt themselves and their own situations to be unique. As far as he could tell, neither Liz nor Harold had any idea that either of them was being considered for election as president of Eastland.

Since these folks were veterans of management seminars, he decided to give them an exposure they had never had before. He called a friend who ran a movie studio and made some arrangements.

8

Class Introduction: "A Day at the Movies"

First Impressions

Ed looked at his five pupils seated around the conference table. This was to be their only common session as things were currently planned. After this, they would each spend time working one-on-one with Ed. He had hoped that more could be done in group sessions, but during the initial interviews there had been little enthusiasm expressed for such activities. However, one never knew what people were going to do once they got into a situation. They seemed to be getting along well at this moment. Initial meetings always reminded him of dogs walking around each other stiff-legged and cautious.

"We need to set down a few foundation bricks," he said. "So I've written four items on this flip chart. They will serve as our beginning. I doubt that there are any more. If we could put together the leader's job description, it would be something like this."

1. Create the right environment—on purpose.
2. Reduce complex issues to something each person can understand and learn to handle.
3. Concentrate on the objectives of the operation.
4. Relate to people at all times.

Nick Winston shifted in his chair and dropped his pencil noisily on the table. Patience had never been one of Nick's assets, but in his case it usually worked to his advantage because he had gained a reputation for getting things done quickly.

"This sounds like a management book already," he growled. "I thought we were going to be a few levels above such things."

Ed wrinkled his brow and scowled at Nick.

"This course is for grown-ups, Nick. I only agreed to take you on the presumption that you were seriously trying to become an executive. We are going to discuss anything to any depth necessary, and all subjects are eligible to be put before the group. But petulance and poor manners are not appropriate. If that doesn't fit with your plan, then you might want to leave now."

There was a pause.

"I didn't mean anything personal, Ed," said Nick. "I guess that's just my way of talking about things."

"Everything is personal, Nick," replied Ed. "Everything is personal. People don't separate things into categories like that. You say it, they register it."

Elizabeth shook her head.

"I think I don't agree with that, Ed," she said. "I think people take things one way in the work place and another in their regular lives. They can tell the difference."

"They shouldn't have to tell the difference," said Ed, "and that is part of creating the proper environment. If you have a make-believe world in the office, you get make-believe reactions."

"And make-believe work?" asked Nick.

"And make-believe work," answered Ed.

"What do you mean by that?" asked Alvin. "Do you really think business is a make-believe world? That would be frightening. I mean I know that a lot of what we do is for effect, but a great deal of reality happens."

Elizabeth agreed.

"Are you serious?" she asked Ed.

Anna raised her hand.

"People don't act at home the way they do in an office. I mean at home they don't sit down and do jobs; they don't go to lunch at a certain time; they don't act polite to people they can't stand. It really is different."

"The workplace certainly is more artificial in many respects," commented Harold. "But there are only a few people involved at home, and they know each other well. Also, they're not necessarily involved in common interests outside of living together."

Liz smiled.

"Also, I think no one is really in charge at home like in the office. People get a lot more latitude in managing their own lives."

"And you can leave a job whenever you want, with no need to look back—something not easily done in a family," said Nick.

"So," nodded Alvin, "we're not really serious about installing a family atmosphere in a company. If we do, it will remove much of the authority of the leadership and put the executive in the same situation as poor old dad."

"Or Mom," Liz added.

Everyone laughed. They were beginning to get comfortable with each other. Ed observed that most of the stiff-legged action had disappeared.

"To See Ourselves as Others See Us"

"Well, there are lots of ways of doing this sort of thing," Ed said. "What kind of environment do you people create in your organizations? Do you do something on purpose, or does what happens happen? Before we get into a discussion on that, I think it would be a good idea to take a look at what's going on now. Then we can get a better idea of what is *real* and what is something else."

"How can we 'take a look at what's going on now'?" asked Anna. "All we would have would be our own opinions, and those may be somewhat biased."

"We're in a wonderful new world of technology and imagination," said Ed. "I have created windows into your organizations. We will watch what goes on through the magic of a VCR. In short, I wrote up what I saw, and we filmed it with actors."

"Saw? Saw where?" asked Elizabeth.

"Inside your organization, that's where," said Ed. "I watched what was going on, talked to people, reviewed results, and made a video. That way we can have a view that we might not obtain otherwise."

"But I haven't noticed anyone doing any filming around our shop," said Nick. "I don't understand what you're talking about."

"He has written us into a movie, Nick," said Harold. "Actors will be playing your people and perhaps even you as your people see you, not as you see you. Those are a lot of 'sees' and 'yous,' but I think that's the idea."

"Right," said Ed. "I realize that we're not going to recreate life exactly as it is, but I couldn't think of any other way to help you know what kind of environment is created by the policies, attitudes, and witnessing each of you expresses."

Nick cleared his throat.

"I've always spent a lot of time stroking my folks and trying to build a team. But I have to say that I think we can get so involved in 'environment creating' that we forget we're supposed to do some work now and then."

Ed was beginning to grow a little irritated with Nick's attitude.

"Okay," he said. "Let's begin with you, Nick, and see how good your 'stroking' and 'creating' are and what results they

bring. I'll turn on the VCR and ask for everyone's comments
after the film is over. It only runs a few minutes. Now don't
forget the people are actors. They're just reciting the lines we
wrote for them."

Nick's World:
Rule of the Bottom Line

VOICE-OVER: The scene is a conference room at the electronics division of Marlot. The program team responsible for developing consumer electronics products is
engaged in a meeting. The subject is the potential acquisition of a small company that produces a unique
semiconductor chip. The code name of the company is
Bravo.

PROGRAM MANAGER: Before we go any further on this
deal, I want to hear from engineering that this family
of chips Bravo has is exactly what we need. And I want
a guarantee from you guys that we'll have a market
edge for a couple of years anyway.

ENGINEERING: They're just what we need, at least right
now. But who knows whether someone in a garage
somewhere isn't coming up with something better?
You know how things happen in this business. We
can't give a guarantee like that.

PROGRAM MANAGER: I don't care "how things happen in
this business." We're not going to lay out all that
dough and then find we're obsolete or outgunned. Finance, how do you feel about the price?

FINANCE: Twenty-six million dollars seems to be appropriate. We've had the investment bankers in on it, and
they're willing to sign a letter of fairness.

PROGRAM MANAGER: Big deal. We need something stronger than that. Can't we show that they wanted a lot
more and we got them down to this level? I mean this

is not a big company we're buying, and there are only four people plus a venture concern involved in the ownership. None of the employees have any stock. These guys held it all to themselves.

FINANCE: What happens to their facilities and people when we take over?

LEGAL: We've promised that they will remain autonomous for at least three years unless there is some major business problem. So the people will all stay in their jobs.

PROGRAM MANAGER: I wouldn't plan on that. The boss will come up with a "business problem" within a few weeks, and we'll absorb the whole product line in the Westville plant.

LEGAL: He said that?

PROGRAM MANAGER: Not in so many words, but that's the only way I can see that we'll be able to cut the expenses enough to fit into his timetable.

HUMAN RESOURCES: How about the employees? Bravo has about 400 people, I think.

PROGRAM MANAGER: We'll keep the engineers who want to stay with us and dump the rest of the people. The patents all come along with the deal, and there is some special equipment.

ENGINEERING: There are about 24 people we would like to have, but I suspect that several of them will want to go out on their own.

LEGAL: All of them are signing noninterference and noncompete contracts as part of the deal, so we can move against them in court if they even come close to the current product. They would have a lot of trouble if they did.

MANUFACTURING: I thought this was supposed to be a friendly takeover. You guys sound like those Wall Street movies. Is the management of Bravo going to continue to run it?

PROGRAM MANAGER: Not for long. They're expensive guys, and they're all going to be well-off from the stock sale. You people don't seem to understand that we have to make back our investment in this acquisition very quickly. Headquarters is going to watch it very closely; and if we stumble, then we'll be in deep doo doo. We need to cut overhead quickly in order to start covering the "good-will" costs.

HUMAN RESOURCES: We can look around inside the corporation to see if anyone needs these people. Some of them are valuable I'm sure.

PROGRAM MANAGER: Oh, don't do that. Everyone will get tipped off. We have to watch the bottom line before everything else. Nick always says "the bottom line is the top priority." He will have our heads if we bring a lot of fat along with these new products.

END

Everyone looked at Nick, who was livid. He stood up and glared at Ed.

"Where in heaven's name did you get that kind of dialogue? We don't act that way in our division. We've made several acquisitions without that sort of attitude. That discussion was unethical as well as not very good business. Why would you start all this off with something as phony as that?"

Ed smiled and reached into his briefcase.

"Here," he said, laying a folder in front of Nick. "This contains the minutes of the meeting we took the dialogue from. It is almost word for word. You got a copy. Don't you remember it?"

Nick thumbed through the folder as the rest of the class sat entranced. Then he glanced up.

"I remember the memo, but I looked at it as if the program manager was just trying to move the team along quicker. All of those things are not to be taken seriously. People need motivation in order to get the acquisition done on time. It costs money to delay.

"But I don't know how they got the idea that I would put the bottom line way ahead of people or of our corporate word on an agreement."

"It must be because that's what they think is the most important part of the business to you," said Ed. "This is the environment we were talking about. One way or another it has been created and biased in that direction. Does anyone have any other ideas on how people might come to that conclusion since Nick obviously doesn't feel that way?"

Harold cleared his throat.

"I have personally had a great deal of difficulty with this environment-creating business. People watch their leader very closely and make up their own minds as to what is important. I've never been able to shake people's opinion that I am primarily concerned with profit even though I've gone out of my way to show my concern for the individual employee."

"People go by what you talk about all the time," said Anna. "What do you talk about all the time, Nick?"

Out of the mouths of babes, thought Ed.

Nick had begun to recover his composure.

"I guess I do emphasize financials," he said, "but I don't mean it to be at the expense of everything else. Those people sounded like a SWAT squad. I'm going to have to think about this in order to put things in the proper perspective. I need a little time to respond. But I do recognize that something has to change."

"Well, that's a beginning," said Ed. "Let's run another tape. This one is from Elizabeth's marketing operation at Eastland. It concerns a sales meeting held last month in the midwest. The people involved are salespeople. They're talking about the seminar which was run by corporate marketing. Do you remember that seminar, Elizabeth?"

"I sure do," she replied. "I wasn't there myself, but the feedback has all been very positive. We're going to do a lot more of them."

Ed pushed the play button on the VCR.

Elizabeth's World:
The Head-in-the-Sand
School of Management

VOICE-OVER: The scene is a coffeehouse in the midst of the loop in Chicago. Three Eastland salespeople have gathered for their weekly coffee chat.

EVELYN: What a bunch of turkeys!

JIM: They must have thought we just got into this business last week or something. I can't believe they dug up that old routine of the steps in a sales call. I went through that 15 years ago.

CAROL: Yeah. I was hoping we could learn more about the new products and how they can help the customer. I find it hard to keep up on that.

JIM: It sure changes fast. We've been having an evening session at Harry's house each month. He has an inside track to the development people. They give him operating and installation information that we can't seem to get from marketing.

EVELYN: Why do you suppose the corporate people think we're completely uneducated in sales? They act like we just got into the business.

JIM: Who do they think has been selling this stuff all these years? Where do they think it goes?

CAROL: My favorite part was when she asked us to list our biggest problems and then turned the list around to the salesperson's "traditional" faintness of heart about making sales calls.

JIM: I really think she doesn't know that every call we make is by appointment in response to a request by the potential client. We're invited in the door.

EVELYN: We don't have to grovel our way in.

CAROL: Or beg for "just one moment."

EVELYN: Have you ever seen any of the corporate marketing staff out on the road? Any at all?

JIM: Elizabeth, the big marketing boss, gets out regularly. She seems to know pretty much what's going on, but her staff doesn't have a glimmer. They get it all out of books or from some magazine, I guess.

CAROL: Like Evelyn said, "What a bunch of turkeys!"

END

It was Elizabeth's turn to be speechless. Recovering herself, she managed to croak that she was certainly surprised by this rendition.

"Is it true?" asked Nick.

"Down to the last Danish," said Ed.

"But how could this be?" asked Elizabeth. "How could there be so much difference between what I heard about the seminar and this coffee conversation? Is someone fooling me, or do they just not know?" She sat down heavily.

"What did the people who gave the seminar say?" asked Harold. "Did they have the class fill out rating forms? Perhaps we could compare the difference on specifics?"

"I don't have them with me, of course," said Elizabeth, "but as I remember the rating summary, most remarks were favorable. I certainly would have remembered if we had received an evaluation like those folks put forth," she replied.

"Have you actually sat through the content of the seminar, Elizabeth?" asked Anna. "Do you know what they're teaching?"

Elizabeth blushed.

"I have to admit that I haven't done that," she said. "I've been so busy on other things I just let myself assume that the staff knew what they were doing. And outside of the comments of the three attendees, I still don't know what did or didn't happen. However, it isn't possible to do everything yourself. How about that, Ed? Should I have checked the content of the seminar personally? Is that executive work?"

"Content, no; concepts, yes," said Ed.

"The staff needs to have a clear picture of what message needs to come across," he continued. "They should be able to work out the details, but the concepts have to fit in with everything else that's happening.

"For instance, I remember when one of my kids went to driver's education in high school. The insurance companies would discount the cost of coverage if new drivers took the course. Well, he took it, graduated, and then passed his state driver's license test."

Harold was puzzled.

"What has that got to do with Elizabeth's seminar?"

"Everything," said Ed. "When I took a ride with him, I discovered that he knew very little about driving the car. During that 10-week course he had about 15 minutes behind a wheel. My first awareness came when he had to parallel park."

"So the concept of the course," said Anna, "was to pass the license examination, not to learn how to be a safe and efficient driver?"

"Exactly," said Ed. "They had completely lost the purpose of the course and what their students needed to learn. There was no discussion of maintenance, vehicle handling, or such. There was very little actual road time. It was mostly movies and lectures. The school executives and the insurance company people think the kids are learning to manage an automobile. The poor old parents are the ones who have to take on that teaching chore."

"So," mused Elizabeth, "the course was set up based on someone's saying, 'We need to teach the new drivers to pass the license examination.' Their thought would have been that passing that test indicated a person would be a good driver."

"Yet we know for a fact," commented Nick, "that everyone now driving has obtained a license and that there are some terrible drivers out there."

"Which means," volunteered Anna, "that there is probably little relationship between the test and driving competence."

"So what did you say to your staff about needing a sales-persons' seminar, Elizabeth?" asked Ed.

She blushed again.

"Well, in thinking about it, what I said was something like 'We need to help the salespeople to learn to sell better.' What I should have said was, 'We need to find out what the sales-people need in order to build effective relationships with the customers.' Then we would probably have found the right content."

"It would seem to me that the executive might take a direct role in such a seminar, such as preparing the agenda or in-terviewing salespeople to get an idea of what is needed," said Harold.

"It might be necessary to do that in order to put the con-cept together," said Ed. "But it mostly depends on the man-agers involved. If they have no experience in such things, then it will take direct involvement to get it all laid out. But normally a clear, one-page charter would be enough. Other-wise, one might as well do it himself."

Harold raised his hand.

"Did you do one in my shop? I'm beginning to imagine all kinds of horror stories. We try to do things properly, but I'm becoming confused about what 'properly' is. When direction is conceived with one thought in mind and implemented with quite another, then it seems to me that this business of being an executive is more complex than I have thought to date."

"I'm with you," said Anna. "Telling people what to do and then deciding if they did it or not never seemed very difficult to me. But I can see that I've been more of a Scout leader than an executive. I've been giving it out in a wrapped pack-age. I'm beginning to think I don't know as much about this stuff as I thought."

"You all have at least one consideration in common," said Ed. "It goes with the territory. Leaders have to be smarter than the average bear. They have to be able to comprehend situations quickly, take on a large load of data without much trouble, think longer-term than others, and be able to trans-late thought into action.

"Yet these are not necessarily the characteristics of an intellectual, and leaders often do not have to fit into that classification. But they have to be knowledgeable, smart, and decisive. All of you are smart; that much I know. The rest remains to be seen."

"But there is more than 'smart,' isn't there?" asked Alvin. "My boss can take a 30-page report, thumb through it, and pick out the only two errors in it. That's more than smart; it's intuition or something."

"It's learned concentration," replied Ed. "You can walk a familiar path through the woods, for instance, and never really notice much about it. But if you take a half dozen Cub Scouts along and you're responsible for their safety, then each hazard will leap up into your consciousness.

"When a report is coming out that's going to be read carefully by others, it's possible to see errors right through the cover."

"I think I've gathered enough courage to see my video now, Ed," said Anna. "What is it about?"

Ed smiled.

"It's about systems, Anna. It's about systems."

Anna's World:
Innovation at All Costs

VOICE-OVER: The scene is the back office of the branch bank. An employee has been transferred to the bank from another branch and is going to be responsible for handling and distributing the branch's mail. She is being oriented by her supervisor, Alex.

ALEX: We have our own post office box. The key is kept here in this drawer. You'll need to pick up the mail a few times a day.

HELEN: How do I go get it?

ALEX: You just drive down there. It's only three blocks away.

HELEN: I don't have a car. My husband drops me off on his way to work and my sister picks me up in the evening.

ALEX: We have a bank car—that little white station wagon you can see out the window. My secretary keeps the keys. You can use it.

HELEN: Couldn't we ask the post office to just deliver it now and then?

ALEX: They don't empty post office boxes and deliver.

HELEN: At the other branch we didn't have a box. They just brought us four or five sacks of mail during the day.

ALEX: Well, we do it this way here. Now when you get the mail, it's sorted over here and placed in these boxes.

HELEN: Then people come and get it?

ALEX: No, you'll deliver it to them. All the mail that looks like it has money in it goes to the head teller. Everything else will most likely be addressed to someone specific. You take it to them.

HELEN: Okay. But that sure is different. I've worked at three separate branches. The bank was nice enough to let me transfer when my husband and I moved, and the system here is different from the other ones.

ALEX: Our boss is an innovator. She's always finding new ways to do things. That's why she's one of the up-and-coming executives in the bank. The big bosses like to show her off to visitors.

HELEN: That's wonderful. I like it when women get recognized. All I was saying is that the system here is a lot more work, and there is a lot more potential to mix things up. But I want to do what you all want to do. When I get this work done, will I have the opportunity to do other jobs, too?

ALEX: I doubt that you'll have any time left. Everyone who has had this job says it takes all day and a little more.

HELEN: Doing it this way, I can see that would be so. I was hoping to have the chance to learn some other things.

ALEX: We'll see.

END

"That wasn't so bad, Anna," said Harold. "Sounds like the new woman needs to get her feet wet a little bit. She doesn't understand your system."

"I invented that mail system myself," said Anna. "I had no idea that the one everyone else used was more efficient. I never even looked."

"Why do you suppose no one ever said it was a problem before?" asked Nick.

"They probably didn't know it could be better either," said Elizabeth.

Anna was thinking about it. Ed waited patiently.

"There has been a nagging thought in the back of my mind for some time. I'm finding it more difficult to get objective comments on the things I do. People treat me differently than they used to," said Anna.

"That's what I call the 'wonder woman' syndrome," commented Elizabeth.

"What in heaven's name is that?" asked Alvin. "Are we supposed to recognize it?"

"I don't think so," said Elizabeth. "I made it up. But it's descriptive." She looked at Anna who was nodding.

"When a woman, particularly a young one like Anna, is discovered to be bright and effective, men tend to be surprised. So she gets a lot of attention and capabilities that she may or may not really have are attributed to her," said Elizabeth.

The men immediately began to disclaim this trait, but Elizabeth's gesture silenced them.

"I can finish, Elizabeth," said Anna. "So what happens is that in a little while she becomes infallible, even when she isn't. So everyone kept on using my mail system because they thought I must know something they didn't."

"I hate to disappoint you," said Nick, "but the same thing applies to men. I've been 'wonder man' for a few years now. Fortunately, I'm so wonderful that it dawned on me in time to build a protective strategy. However, as you saw in our first film, people will march straight into the jaws of foolishness if they think that's what I want."

"I'm glad you all picked this up," Ed remarked. "It's a tip-of-the-iceberg analysis. When people stop thinking, it means that the executive has somehow flipped their switch. To put it another way, if they think you're going to think of it, they don't have to think of it, so they don't."

"Boy, that's a mouthful," said Elizabeth, "but I get the point. Does that mean that each executive needs to invest in a barrel in order to hide the proverbial light?"

"I don't know if *hide* is the correct word, but it's a thought. People can be overpowered," noted Ed.

"But I've seen the same result with 'dumb,'" said Harold. "When people think the boss is incapable of recognizing a good idea, they will also keep quiet about a need to do something."

"A well-taken point," said Ed. "The difference is that smart people usually recognize they're smart and can shelter it a little. Dumb people don't realize they're dumb, so they get into everything."

"Who's next on this 'March of Time'?" asked Nick.

"A day in the life of Harold Clark, coming up," said Ed.

Harold's World: Ad Hoc as Policy

VOICE-OVER: The weekly meeting of the loan committee of Eastland Finance. This group approves or disapproves applications provided by district offices. Normally, they only deal with contracts of over $50,000 and credit lines in excess of $100,000, leaving deals under those amounts to the discretion of the local manager. Attendees usually include the chief financial officer, the credit manager, the executive vice president, the regional executive, and Harold. Harold was not in attendance on this day.

CFO: This is an easy session. There are four renewals of credit lines and one new one. You all received the information on the renewals and know that these people have been with us for years and have never disappointed us even a little bit.

CREDIT: I wish we had several hundred like these.

CFO: May I have a motion to renew all four?

REGIONAL: Let me ask a question before we vote on these, and I hasten to say that they're all great deals both for us and for them. We have a problem in the field offices, and these lines are good examples.

EXECUTIVE VP: What problem?

REGIONAL: Interest rates. Here we have four deals, all with the same usage and repayment record, all in the same neighborhood as far as amount goes.

EXECUTIVE VP: So?

REGIONAL: So, they all have different interest rates. They range from 1 percent over prime rate to 4 percent over. Two are adjustable, depending on the prime, and two are fixed.

CFO: What's the problem?

REGIONAL: Actually, there are two problems. The first is that we don't make the same amount of money on all of them. In fact, one is marginal. The second problem is that our people don't know what to tell potential customers about the interest rates. We need a policy on it.

CREDIT: I think the policy is to get whatever they will put up with.

CFO: Not exactly, but it works out that way.

REGIONAL: Well, look at this proposed new line. Here is an automobile dealer who wants a 21-million-dollar revolving line of credit. If he goes to a bank, they have it posted in the window and will negotiate from that. I realize that it can change every day, but that's what fax machines are for. We need a policy.

EXECUTIVE VP: Harold wants us to keep these things loose.

REGIONAL: I can see the value of that, but I think we need to give our people better guidance.

CREDIT: What would you suggest?

REGIONAL: Well, there is a board in London that meets each morning to decide what the price of gold should be that day, worldwide. And as soon as they say a number, everyone in the world buys and sells at that number—no complaints. I don't see why this group can't do the same thing once a week.

EXECUTIVE VP: Set the price of gold? Okay, okay, just kidding.

CREDIT: We could set how much over prime the floating rate would be and provide a specific number for the fixed rate.

CFO: Quit dreaming. Harold will never go for that. He wants to do it on a one-customer-at-a-time basis.

REGIONAL: Customers are beginning to wonder about us.

CFO: May I have a show of hands on these four contracts?

END

"I remember a radio show once," said Alvin, "where two guys opened a parking lot and couldn't agree on what to charge, so they decided to get whatever they could get. Then one day, a friend watched the lot for them. They told him to get whatever he could get. When they came back, he handed them $400 and said he had sold the Ford over in the corner."

"I guess I see the point of the film and the story," said Harold. "But I never thought that policies were all that important when you had people who were capable of making a judgment."

"Don't you think they need guidelines at least?" asked

Anna. "I would think that people would be frustrated if they had to make those decisions that can come back to bite them in the future."

"One of the people in the film said a contract was 'marginal.' What does that mean?" asked Nick.

"It refers to a fixed-rate line of credit that's sitting right at prime now. If the prime rises, and it looks like the way things are going, then we have to explain to the boss why earnings are low or flat on that contract—" answered Harold, "no one's favorite job, particularly if it could turn into a loss."

"That's the whole idea of a rate policy," said Ed. "If necessary, people can negotiate specific deals, but at least they're beginning from a standard base. Also, in some cases it's possible to be accused of taking advantage of a customer."

"I'll think about it," said Harold. "But I'm not convinced that it's an essential part of our business."

Alvin's World: Chaos on the Quality Front

VOICE-OVER: Each quarter the Estate corporation has a suppliers' quality meeting. Representatives of companies who provide products or services to Estate are asked to attend. At those meetings Estate's quality status is discussed, and suppliers are encouraged to bring up any problems they have in delivering products and services. The meeting is being conducted by the deputy purchasing director and the staff quality representative.

PURCHASING: Now that everyone has been introduced and we've seen the quality film from our chairman, I would like to open the floor to questions. Bring up anything you like.

SUPPLIER ONE: Our people have asked me to bring up the subject of the statistical-process control charts. We have to send in charts from our operation every week, but we never hear anything about them. Our questions are: What happens to the charts? Should we consider everything to be okay if we don't hear anything?

QUALITY: We look at all of them and make comments. If you haven't received any comments, then yours must be all right. Of course, there are a great many coming in all the time. Right now, we're a little behind.

SUPPLIER TWO: Have you ever had any that showed a process was out of control?

QUALITY: I can't think of any right at this moment.

SUPPLIER ONE: Do you think anyone would send out a chart that showed the operation was out of control?

QUALITY: I doubt it.

SUPPLIER TWO: Then why do you insist on these charts being sent in? It costs a lot of extra money, and we have to do it in areas in which we normally would not consider it useful.

QUALITY: We just want to be certain that our suppliers are taking care about their processes.

PURCHASING: We'll take a look at this requirement. Are there any other questions?

SUPPLIER THREE: We make fittings, and our experience with Estate is that they send out purchase requests to a dozen suppliers and then take the one with the lowest bid. It's hard to build a relationship when it's based only on price.

PURCHASING: Price is important.

SUPPLIER THREE: Well, we can meet most prices, but we would like to think that delivery and quality fit into the equation also. Frankly, we're thinking about not responding to Estate's requests under these conditions.

PURCHASING: Well, there are a lot of other people who like our business.

END

Ed turned off the video player.

"It gets a little messy after that," he said.

"This is supposed to be a friendly and encouraging meeting," said Alvin. "We rehearsed all the presentations, hired a consultant, made special films, tried to do everything right."

"Those two didn't seem to be too clear on how to answer questions," said Nick. "They might have been stoned to death before it was all over."

"They seem to have forgotten the purpose of the meeting, which, I assume, was to help the suppliers do better by Estate," said Elizabeth.

"That's what it was supposed to be," said Alvin. "But as I think back, we never said that clearly. It was assumed."

Adjourned

There was a long silence. Finally Nick spoke up.

"I think we should have a few more of these group sessions if for no other reason than to let us each discover that we aren't the only ones who don't understand the art of becoming an executive. I feel better about everything."

Others echoed Nick's comment.

"Okay," said Ed. "We'll do that later. Right now I'm scheduled to spend some time with each of you individually. During those sessions I want to deal with what you're working on at that time. We'll go as deep as we must to see if things are going the way they should.

"I will look forward to seeing you in your own caves."

9

Elizabeth

Some Tough Lessons in Relating

"We were just beginning to work with the Smeldon Company, and I wanted to make certain that everything started off right. So I set up a trip to go to their headquarters and then to a couple of facilities," said Elizabeth.

"I imagine everyone was pleased that you wanted to do that," said Ed.

"Enthusiastic, enthusiastic," she replied. "One of the reasons they decided to go with us was that this convinced them they would get the personal attention they think they need. So we're going to give them a lot of it. Their CEO, Charlie Hope, wants constant reassurance. Sometimes I wonder how he got such a big job."

"So how did you go about planning the trip?"

"I called Charlie personally and asked him who he wanted me to deal with. He assigned his personal assistant to make the arrangements. I wanted to see if we could do it all in two days, one overnight. I hate to be away from the kids."

"How far are the facilities from their headquarters?" asked Ed.

"A two-hour flight. So I figured I could arrive in Chicago

in the morning, have lunch with Charlie and his team, walk around headquarters once, and then fly to the location... dinner that night, a tour in the morning, lunch with some of the nonmanagement people, then home by 5 P.M. It would be a lot of running around but well worth it."

"And that's the way it all came off?"

"Well, not exactly. I got to their headquarters and went to Charlie's office. He was tied up, so they took me on a tour of the marketing and computer areas. He didn't show up until halfway through lunch. But we had a nice chat, and I got off on time to fly out to the operation.

"I was able to make a few points about our company and the support we were going to supply, but I was disappointed that we didn't have more time together."

"And how did things go at the operation?"

"Pretty good. I had dinner with the general manager and his wife as well as the human resources director. They were interested in talking about the experiences other companies had had in implementing our services. I was surprised that they didn't know more about it. That made things a little touchy. Also, it was a little difficult having his wife there. I got the feeling she didn't really approve of women doing serious work in business."

"Should they have known more?" asked Ed.

"I would think so. The program was bought through headquarters, but I had assumed that they talked to each other about it. Anyway, I was able to fill them in on most of it. They seemed anxious to get started." She poured herself another cup of coffee.

"And the tour?"

"Very useful. I have a much better idea of the real work that goes on in the company. You would never realize it from being in their headquarters. I think those at headquarters haven't the slightest idea what's happening out there. I'll have to take Charlie out and show him. I was able to point out several actions they can take that will save enough money to pay for all the materials and service we'll be giving them.

"I wrote a short note to Charlie thanking him for the visit and pointing out the cost eliminations I had generated. I figured that would turn him on to us."

"A Turkey of a Trip"

"And was he grateful?" Ed probed.

"Strangely enough," said Elizabeth, "he was very cool about the whole thing when I called him later. In fact, they've slowed down their activity and are postponing getting started. So much for trying to smooth things up front. I'll stick to just doing my job from now on."

"I can see that you have no idea of why that relationship has cooled off," said Ed. "Is that so?"

Elizabeth looked puzzled.

"You don't know anything about it except what I've told you here in a few moments," she said. "You've never met any of these people. You haven't been to the places I've been, and I don't think you even know what it is my company does."

She paused for a breath and nervously picked up a cookie.

"So how," she continued, "could you know if the relationship has cooled and if it has, why it cooled?"

Ed smiled and nodded.

"Did you ever hear the story about the guy who went to the counselor and told him that he didn't get along with anyone and that nobody liked him and that he wanted help? Then while the counselor meditated for a moment, the guy tapped the table with his knuckle and said 'Pay attention while I'm talking to you, stupid.'"

Ed chuckled at his own story, but Elizabeth's face was bright red. She stood up.

"I don't appreciate that at all, Ed," she stormed. "Your little stories are crude sometimes. You should learn to direct them better."

"You gonna put out a contract on me?" asked Ed. "Stories are a good way of talking when a point needs to be made.

Now, do you want to examine this situation or do you want to go tell your boss that he's wasting his money?"

"Well, I don't think I'm like that. You're being unfair." She sat down but was still having difficulty controlling her emotions.

"I'm sorry," Ed said. "I'll try to do better in the future. But you're a very bright, energetic, and ambitious person. If we're going to get you on the path you want to be on, we have to talk turkey." He stood up and walked to the window.

"Now your trip was a turkey, and it's important for you to know why it was a turkey."

He turned to face her.

"You *do* think it was a turkey, don't you?"

Elizabeth put her hands in her lap and lowered her head as she nodded in reluctant agreement.

"Do you have any idea why?" he asked. "Do you have even the tiniest vision of how you appeared to these people?"

"I hope it was as an interested and efficient executive. That's what I am, or what I try to be." She was regaining her composure.

"I'm sure that's what you are. But let's examine for a moment just what you're interested in and efficient at. If you were interested in making certain that the relationship was going to be solid, why didn't you take the key interface person from your company along with you? After all, you don't plan to do the day-to-day work on this contract, do you?" He sat down again across the table and looked at her.

"Of course not. That will be handled by the account executive, who's one of our best. But he was coming out the following week, and it seemed inefficient to have him make two trips."

"Could you have gone when he was going?" asked Ed.

"I suppose so, but it didn't fit my schedule."

"Did you ask him to change his?"

Elizabeth opened her briefcase and took out her calendar.

"Look, doing this at all meant changing things all around. I was trying to be a nice guy and help out. Believe me, that's the last time for that." Ed shook his head and patted her wrist.

"Now just settle down. I think if we reconstruct this whole thing, you'll see what I'm driving at. I don't doubt you had the best of intentions in everything, but you are so self-oriented—perhaps because you want to do especially well—that you're missing the point."

She turned to face him and sternly demanded an answer. "Without telling me any quaint stories just lay it out so I can understand it. What exactly is your point?"

Arrogance? Me?

"The point," said Ed, "is that you come across as being arrogant and only pretending to be interested in other people. Whether that's actually true or not is something we'll have to determine, but that's the way it reads."

Elizabeth was silent for a long moment. Then she shook her head.

"Arrogant? I've busted my tail, given up my private life for this company and my career. I've studied and worked. I've dragged people along to help them improve, and now you say I'm arrogant. And even if I were, what has that got to do with being an effective executive? I would think having confidence in oneself would be an advantage."

Ed grinned and settled in his chair.

"One day, my wife asked me why I didn't play golf with Harry anymore. I asked her if she would want to play with someone who cheated on his score, moved the ball in the rough, and talked while his opponent was playing. She said that she certainly would not. 'Neither will Harry,' I replied."

Elizabeth smiled and began to relax a little.

"So I'm the bad guy but don't recognize it?" she said.

"Hardly bad," replied Ed. "But we have to take a look at your style. It's quite possible to have a negative effect while trying very hard to do things just the opposite.

"Arrogance is one of the primary causes of executive failure, and plain old egotism is right behind it. However, arrogance is curable while egotism may not be.

"People who take over a company and then completely restructure it so it will be theirs are just like the monkey tribes in which the new leader kills all the newborn infants so there won't be any but his around.

"They sell all the existing divisions, buy some new ones, start a couple of other businesses, and then feel safe. However, the monkey tribes usually survive that sort of thing, whereas companies may not.

"The behavior in your case is hardly so radical but is in the same pattern. You called up a client, announced the schedule everyone was going to follow, ordered their CEO about, gossiped about him, and made them all bit players in your personal bid for immortality.

"While making the visit to bolster relationships, you put down the person they are dealing with. They all probably thought the purpose of the whole trip was to bite the head off your own account manager."

A Painful Coming to Terms

Elizabeth was pale now, and for the moment Ed was concerned that she was going to pass out on him.

"Sometimes I get carried away," he said. "Perhaps we should break off this session now and get together later next week."

She raised her hand.

"No, I'm all right," she said. "It's just that you've made me think about all this, and I have to admit that you're right.

"I didn't plan it that way consciously, but I must have wanted to make a big impression on those folks and have them feed back to our management that it was an effective trip. All I did was embarrass the company and perhaps lose us an account.

"How can I get this straight in my head?"

"Well, just thinking about it is a big step," said Ed. "It's very hard to manipulate oneself in different ways for different occasions. Sometimes we can overmanage the whole thing. The key is to avoid having to manage yourselves, just to be natural. 'Be thyself,' to coin a phrase."

Elizabeth thought about that for a moment.

"The natural me is much too mild-mannered to be effective," she said. "I come across as being wimpy, if that's a description that can be applied to women. People just run all over me if I let them."

She was becoming more comfortable with the discussion.

"Pay attention while I'm talking to you, stupid," she laughed.

Ed smiled, too, and relaxed back in the chair.

"Good. Well, I think you may have underestimated the real you, who is perfectly acceptable and charming and effective. Women have certain advantages, you know, and it is fair to use them. One of the advantages is that they're not men. Women don't make good men, no matter how hard they try. And men don't make great women."

He leaned forward and picked at the grapes on the table.

"I have a friend—and this is a true story—who wanted to learn to speak German. However, he was too cheap to take lessons. So he started to date a young German woman, and through the system of "pillow talk" learned to speak the language in a little over a year. Then they broke up, and he went on with his life only to find that he spoke like his girlfriend. If you listen to the phrases women use in ordinary discussion, it is easy to see that there is a difference. The result in his case was that it made people wonder about him when he talked German."

Elizabeth smiled.

"So he wasn't himself. What did he do about it?"

"He pretended he couldn't speak German but could understand it a little. Then he spent his time listening to men talking and doing business. In a little while, he got rid of most of his feminine phrases, but once in a while one pops up. Then he pretends he's teasing."

Cultivating Staywithitness

"So should I listen and watch? Do I put my career on hold during that time and just sit around?"

Elizabeth was getting a little edgy now that they were talking about actually doing something. It was becoming apparent that she could develop a clear case of insecurity if the opportunity presented itself.

But Ed shook his head impatiently.

"Listen yes, but hardly sit around. I want you to get right back in there and turn this story around. You can do it with a little thought and effort. Now what are you going to do specifically? Think about it a moment, and then let's walk through a plan. If you wait three weeks to come up with something, it won't be any better than the one that comes off the top of your head right now."

She cocked her head and looked at him in concern.

"You mean you feel off the top of my head will be better than something I spend three weeks working out? I've always been taught that planning takes time. How do you explain this switch?"

"Planning takes thought, not necessarily time. When people have three weeks to work it out, they don't begin until the time is almost up anyway. What I want is for you to think about it while it has intensity in your mind. You're never going to feel about it the way you do right now.

"In a week you will have rationalized the whole thing and decided that it wasn't that bad after all. No one is ever going to call you on it, but they will have it in the back of their minds, and so will you."

Elizabeth looked at him with growing determination.

"Well, my plan is that I'm going to apologize to Charles and his staff as well as to our account executive. Then I'm going to ask how I can help him with the client.

"Second, I'm going to have a good chat with myself and quit acting like the gal in *The Front Page*. I'm smart, well-educated, experienced, and have made it so far on my own. I like the real me, and that's what I'm going to be.

"Now, what else do I need to work on?"

Ed smiled and patted her on the shoulder.

"Well, at the next session we should be talking about selecting and evaluating people. The first question will be: How do you evaluate yourself, and would you select you to be your boss?"

Elizabeth grimaced.

"Yesterday, I didn't want to have anything to do with myself, but today I'm giving me another chance. We'll see how it looks tomorrow."

"Good enough, see you at the next session." Ed started to leave the room, but Elizabeth intercepted his progress to give him a hug.

"Thanks," she said. "That's something women executives are free to do," and she hurried out.

* * *

The executive needs to help the organization work. Whenever the person with the most power steps into a picture, everyone else pulls back. Foreign policy, for instance, is irresistible to presidents, prime ministers, kings, and such. They will turn over domestic policy to underlings without a quiver. But they place themselves right on the front edge of international relations.

For this reason the Foreign Service never gets very good. They never are permitted to do much more than carry out the orders of the senior executive. The Secretary of State makes grand trips, making grand arrangements, and those who are supposed to be managing such things are left out. The executive becomes the manager.

When President Wilson went off to Europe after the end of World War I, he took with him the peace plan that was ultimately agreed upon. He was the dominant figure of the conference because everyone else was worn out by the four-year conflict. Wilson, representing the new world, projected energy and a positive attitude. The rest went along with his "Fourteen-Points" plan, which sounded like a good approach. However, the harsh terms that were included set

Germany off on a course of internal disruption that laid the foundations for the next war.

Wilson was so confident in the power of his plan and his own personal popularity that he paid no attention to his opposition. He took no one from the Republican party with him to France. As a result, the U.S. Senate rejected the treaty, the United States never became part of the League of Nations, and Wilson had a stroke. Because he did not *let* others, or *help* others, he became unable to govern and was embarrassed to the point of illness.

Harry Truman, when taking part in creating the United Nations, made certain that others were influential in its development. Opposition politicians were appointed to the founding task force, so that the UN enjoyed bipartisan support. Truman had learned from Wilson's experience.

Fence Mending

Elizabeth went to the office of Ernest Whalton, who was assigned as account executive to Smeldon Corporation. She had called ahead to make sure he was free and then walked over. Ernest rose as Elizabeth entered, and she permitted him to seat her at his conference table. She was a little nervous about this visit and about her newfound determination to be herself. After a few informalities, Elizabeth began.

"I wanted to chat about Smeldon and our relationship with them as a client. I feel that I didn't handle my visit there really well and that I may have put you in a poor situation. So I thought we might be able to put together something whereby I can help you get everything back on track. Or, if you wish, I'll just bug out of the whole thing."

"Oh, don't do that," said Ernest. "I can really use your help. They have kind of gone into hibernation for a while, but I think they are realizing that they're only hurting themselves. I have an appointment to see them next week. Would you like to go with me?"

"I would be delighted, but I want to do it as part of a well-thought-out plan."

And so they thought it out. Elizabeth began to realize that she needed to use this activity as a laboratory in order to develop a new "customer-orientation program." It was going to be necessary to recognize that the Eastland personnel and the customer had to develop a common understanding of what was going to happen and how everything would come about.

In the past the person making the initial contact and developing the strategy had backed off from the relationship as soon as the implementation team came into the picture. As a result, much of the early work disappeared and misunderstandings became common. There had to be a way of assuring continuity.

A few days later, Elizabeth and her staff discussed ideas and procedures for developing a new customer-orientation program.

Meeting with the Troops

"Client dropout during the first year is 23 percent," said Elizabeth. "The reasons for this are not always visible; but from what we can learn, it has to do primarily with the clients' feelings that what is happening is not what they thought was going to happen."

"Well that's the fault of the salespeople, Elizabeth," said Harvey. "They make all sorts of promises that we can't keep. We have to fight that all the time."

"The salespeople have to explain our programs right out of the catalog," replied Eleanor. "There isn't any room for inventing things. I'll say that they sometimes don't understand the newer products completely. But I think that's an internal training problem."

"So if it isn't the salespeople and it isn't the account executive's team, then I can only assume that our customers are not very bright," said Elizabeth. "Do we need a program to pick a better class of customers?"

"Okay, I get the message," said Harvey. "I just wanted to make sure that we weren't going out on a witch-hunt like what has happened over the years—not since you took over marketing, Elizabeth, I might hasten to add."

"That was a good 'hasten,' Harvey," remarked Eleanor.

"It won't do any good for any of us to be defensive about this thing," said Elizabeth. "We all have our careers wrapped up in it. So what I want to do is lay out a clear concept of how we bring a new client on board and then how we keep the communication and the results right up-to-date. Clients can find plenty of excuses for changing accounts. There's no reason for us packaging some for them."

All agreed.

"So let's break the relationship down into a few segments." She moved over to the flip chart. "First is client awareness. This is how they find out about us. What parts of that should I put down?"

"Well, most of our responses come either from the institutional ads we put in business magazines or from referrals by other people, mostly clients or exclients. We don't do any direct mail or any cold calls. This way, they are inviting us to come chat with them," said Eleanor.

"Right," said Elizabeth. "So before the sales call is made, we have the opportunity to study the prospective client's history and status. Then sales can get some idea of what preliminary strategies we can propose."

"I've always felt that the initial call should be based primarily on listening just for that reason. Unfortunately, many of our people pour out our whole story all over the client at this time and confuse them," said Harvey.

"Well, that's why we're going to lay out this process," commented Elizabeth. "We need to put ourselves in the most positive situation so we can make the client successful in the long run.

"So I have *client awareness* and *determination of client need* as the first two. Next, I think, is the investigation phase in which we actually go look at the operation and get acquainted."

"That would seem right," said Harvey. "We've always invited them over to see us, and we've gone to one of their locations anyway. However, the question, it seems to me, is more *who* goes than *where* they go. The people to get involved at this stage are the ones who are going to run the account."

"I disagree," said Stan. "I've been listening to all this without comment. But I think we're on the wrong track here. Clients don't want to deal with salespeople. They want to know the ones who are going to do the job. Every time we change people with them, they feel like they are starting all over again."

"So?" asked Elizabeth.

"So," said Stan, "I think we should get rid of salespeople. Let's train them to become account executives, or let's put them in the warehouse, but let's stop jerking the clients around."

"Stan, do you have any idea of the price difference between salespeople and account executives?" asked Eleanor. "Do you know how hard it is to find them? Do you know that it takes a year or more to get them to the point that they are useful? Do you think we want those kinds of folks sitting around waiting rooms?"

"I'm sure the trade-offs are there. We just have to look for them," said Stan.

"Reorganization is not what I have in mind," noted Elizabeth. "There is no advantage to making a bigger problem to solve an existing situation. All we're after here is a road map that will let everyone know where they are traveling. Now stick with me and it will all come clear, I hope."

Elizabeth wrote on the chart.

"This is where I see us heading. These are the phases in the client relationship. We'll need to develop each of them in order to know who is going to do what:

• Client awareness

• Determination of client need

• Orientation visits (home and home)

• Preliminary strategy

• Strategy and contract

- Execution
- Maintenance and upgrading
- Status reviews

"So if we agree on this list, then we have to lay out which part of the organization is specifically responsible for accomplishing each component. It's very important that nothing slip in between them."

"To do that each of those steps will need a written description of action along with some procedures, as well as training to make it all happen. This could be a big job, Elizabeth," said Stan.

"It could cost a lot of money," nodded Harvey.

Elizabeth looked puzzled.

"Isn't that what we're supposed to do anyway? Aren't we supposed to lay out the plan, describe the requirements, and teach the people to do it?"

"No one from higher up has said we're supposed to get into this sort of thing in this much detail. We might be getting off into an area where we're not supposed to go," said Eleanor.

Elizabeth nodded. Suddenly, she was beginning to remember some of the things that Ed had said. She smiled reassuringly to the group and said: "Well, this is the track we're going to take. I'll assign the work on a phase-by-phase basis to several of you; and when the early work is done, we'll bring the complete operation together in order to lay out the nuts and bolts. Stan, I want you to be the program manager on this.

"We're going to get ourselves organized so that we're more effective, but most of all we're going to reduce that client dropout rate to zero. Thank you for coming."

When she returned to her office, Elizabeth placed a call to Ed. His recording machine answered and encouraged her to leave a message.

"Ed," she recorded, "I finally understand the difference between being an executive and being a manager."

10
Nick

Initiating Major Corporate Strategy

Nick welcomed Ed at his office door and led the older man into the conference area of the room. After they were seated, Nick leaned forward and smiled.

"I have to tell you, Ed, that I wasn't too thrilled with the idea of this involvement at first. But I also have to say that it has made a big difference in the way I look at things. I may turn out to be an executive yet."

"I'd be interested in the kinds of things you're favoring with a different view. Are they primarily operational or administrative?" Ed asked.

"Operational, I guess. Frankly, it's not that easy to tell the difference anymore. Operational and administrative used to be two different worlds. Now they intertwine. I don't make any differentiation. Anyway, I've made our ethical policy very clear—a communication not all that easy to get across, I might add. Apparently I gave the impression that I was in favor of robbing orphanages if that would enable us make our numbers. I'm afraid it isn't over yet. Stamping out my 'Jesse James' reputation might take a while.

"Also, I'm starting to get more involved in understanding

financial management. I'm realizing that money is the blood supply of an organization, not just its food."

"Good analogy," said Ed. "An organization is a body, and every part has to be nourished. What have you been thinking about specifically? Sometimes it's hard to get organizations to feed on the right things."

An Unsettling Trip to the Field

Nick rose, walked over to his desk, and returned with a folder. He opened it and selected a few notes.

"I went up to the Westville plant the other day, unannounced, and persuaded Jim Anderson just to let me wander around the place by myself. I had to promise that I would not tell anyone to do anything about anything.

"A few of the people recognized me as I went around, but to most of them I was just another guy in a suit. Over in the machine shop I stopped by a computer-driven mill that was shut down for repairs. The worker didn't seem to mind my looking over his shoulder, so I did. After a moment or two, he turned to me and held up a small bearing unit.

"'Here's the trouble,' he said. 'All jammed up. The lubrication has disappeared.'

"'Where was it made?' I asked. 'That's a pretty essential component.'

"'Oh, it isn't the bearing's fault,' he replied. 'It just hasn't been lubricated. These things work at high speed and under a lot of heat. Someone has to be checking the oil regularly. We don't do much of that around here.'

"I was confused.

"'I thought we had a preventive maintenance program to take care of all that,' I said. 'Wouldn't this sort of thing come under that program?' He just smiled at me.

"'Prevention is not something they think about now, mister. It costs money that doesn't go right to the bottom line. The whole place is having problems or will pretty soon.'

"I thanked him and wandered on. In the receiving area,

boxes were piled on the floor or on forklift pallets. Inspectors and expediters were looking through the cartons and accompanying paperwork. I stood watching until one of them noticed me and asked if she could help.

"'Thanks,' I answered. 'I'm just trying to get an idea of what goes on in this area. It is receiving inspection, isn't it?' She nodded and pointed with her free arm.

"'The material comes in through that dock over there, the boxes are stacked here, and then we look through them to find the most urgent so they can get checked and moved into stores. Unfortunately, these days almost everything is urgent, so we have to do a lot of expediting. These other people are inspectors. I find things for them to inspect.'

"'This is all part of the quality department, I assume,' I said.

"'Used to be, but now it works for purchasing. That way it's all supposed to be more efficient and less expensive.'

"'The inspectors work for purchasing, too?'

"'Sure, the whole receiving department does. One thing's for sure—it cuts down on the rejections. We use about everything we get now. The purchasing manager can accept the defects that are considered unimportant, and that has speeded the system up.'

"'I would think so,' I stated. 'How does everyone feel about this?'

"'Well, it depends on where you're sitting. Around here, it's cut down the hassle a lot, but the fabrication people are not too thrilled. They have to do a lot more inspection than before. They get a lot of stuff they can't use.'

"She smiled and returned to her work and waved as I thanked her. I went through the door to Engineering.

"My first exposure to an engineering department was in a summer job during college. The place was full of drafting tables, and everyone was quite adept at drawing out the details of products the company made. But now, drafting tables are hard to find. People sit in little cubicles peering into a computer.

"Using a wand instead of a pencil, they can draw something, test it out, figure all the tolerances and other mathematics, drive it 100,000 miles, and never leave the booth. Software programs check up on software programs, and a great deal of inefficiency has been removed.

"Three engineers were in the coffee room as I entered, and they all recognized me. As they introduced themselves and poured me a cup of coffee, I realized that they were all a good bit younger than I. Perhaps my 'boy wonder' days are coming to an end.

"We chatted about the business for a while, and then I asked them routinely, 'What's your biggest problem?'

"With many smiles and much chattering they kidded about that for a while until one of them finally responded.

"'I guess it's wondering about the future of the work here. Are we going to be in business much longer?'

"I almost went into shock. 'Forever,' I said. 'Our plan is to grow and prosper in electronics. It's the future of our world. One thing we're thinking about is bringing chip manufacturing and software development into this facility. That would give us complete coverage.' They heard me but still looked puzzled.

"'But we've heard that all the budgets are being cut,' said one. 'That sounds like the future is dim rather than glowing.'

"'Budgets are always getting cut,' I said. 'Sometimes I think that's what they're for. However, we'll be pouring a lot of money into Westville and other areas in the division. Electronics is something the world can't do without.'

"'That sure is good to hear, Mr. Winston,' said the engineer. 'We've been concerned that we might have to move. This area is a good place to live, and this has been a fine place to work.'

"They all excused themselves to return to work, and I continued my tour. However, by this time I was becoming somewhat depressed and was concerned that my face or my demeanor might begin to show it. So I returned to the office area and sat in the conference room with one more cup of coffee. Jim Anderson soon joined me.

"'Well, how was your tour?' he asked. 'My feedback so far is that everyone enjoyed seeing you wandering around without a specific agenda. It might be a good thing to do regularly if you find time.'

"I agreed.

"'I think I'll find time for it in the future,' I said. 'It should be part of every executive's education. Tell me, have we cut back on our preventive maintenance program?'

"'You know we have,' he said. 'At the budget review last spring finance proposed that we reduce our expenditures for long-range things since technology was changing so fast. The idea was that we would be replacing equipment more often anyway, out of necessity. At the same time, everyone was asked to take from 5 to 8 percent out of each functional department budget. It's been a tough task around here, particularly with the growth targets.'

"'Where did the cuts come in?' I asked.

"'I don't know about all of them,' he said. 'We let the functional directors take responsibility for those reductions. In some cases it was necessary for them to combine operations.'

"'Like in receiving inspection?' I asked. He looked at me in a different manner.

"'Boy, you get around. It seems to work out all right, and we were able to eliminate the need for a supervisor and one expediter.'

"'I suspect they also eliminated a shipping clerk, too, because they certainly aren't sending anything back. Has anyone figured what it costs to do the extra inspection out in the fabrication area? I would suspect that compensation there has gone up.'

"'It isn't possible to eliminate without crimping something somewhere. The direction has been a clear assumption that everything is overpriced and should be reduced. I don't agree with it, but we try to do the best we can.'

"'I'm not picking on you or what has happened here. We have to take another look at our strategy and see where we're headed. There's no need to spend a nickel more than we

need to spend, but we have to make certain we're not com-
promising our future,' I responded.

"I patted him on the shoulder and assured him again that
I thought he was running a good shop and that we would get
together again soon. Driving home, I knew I had to do something about our managerial environment. That made me
think of you, and here we are. I think I'm only going to get
one chance to straighten this out and would like to do it
right."

Reevaluating Priorities

"Have you made any decisions about what you want to do?"
asked Ed. "Have you laid out any goals?"

"Well, I know what I want to do," Nick replied. "This organization has to be aimed in the proper direction of profitable growth. That means we do things right, we don't throw
money away, we satisfy our customers, and we lead our industry. That sounds like everyone who gets interviewed by
Fortune, but that's where we need to go."

"I like the word *aim,*" said Ed. "That seems to me to be a
more specific way of setting a goal."

"We could make an acronym out of it like 'Action Is Management,'" said Nick.

"Or, 'Avarice Is Me,'" countered Ed. "Perhaps the world
doesn't need another set of initials. However, *aim* is still a
good word."

"Well, I came back from Westville ready to tear the budgeting process out by the roots. I felt that we were being so
provincial about it all that we were not providing the proper
consideration for the future. I don't want to be one of those
people who becomes known for squeezing every drop of
profit out of an organization and then goes off to better
worlds leaving this down-at-the-heels outfit waiting for plas-
tic surgery," said Nick.

"What did you do?"

"I hauled the financial guy in and asked him why we were

being penny-wise and pound-foolish. He thought that was a good saying. Apparently he hadn't heard it before. We looked at the numbers, and it began to dawn on me that there just is not enough money to go around. We're supporting 6 plants, 32 product lines, a research laboratory, and the division staff. We've acquired several small companies, and that has added to the absorption of money. Corporate supplies the capital, but we have to pay the interest on it until it's paid off." He sat back and sighed.

Ed pursed his lips.

"So it isn't just a bunch of today-oriented, narrow-minded, functional managers making this all happen? And it isn't just a matter of laying out the right operating policies? Then it must be something more," said Ed.

Nick looked up in surprised amusement.

"Why do I get the feeling that you've been waiting patiently for me to discover my problem? You could've saved me a lot of trouble by just letting me know where to look," he said.

"I still don't know if you're looking in the right place or what your plans are. But I do know that you seem a lot more open to taking an objective view of the situation. I'm anxious to hear what's taking shape," replied Ed.

Nick pulled a computer-generated spreadsheet out of the folder and spread it across the table.

"This is a breakout on all of our products and product groups. I've circled the ones that are not contributing their proper share. Until we did this study, I thought I knew what was what. However, it's apparent that several of these are not useful, and some may never be. Yet we've been distributing our resources in a fairly equal fashion across the board. My idea is to get rid of the lines that aren't doing well and concentrate on those which have a future."

Ed ran his finger down the list.

"How are you going to determine that?" he asked. "Sometimes it's hard to tell what's going to be great later on."

Nick agreed.

"However, we can set some criteria. First, it should be a line that's one of the top three in the market while meeting the profitability requirements. Or it can be a new product with agreed potential. The rest have to be sold off or dropped.

"Of the 32 product lines, at least 10 fail to meet one of those tests. Several lines have been around for a long time and are considered part of the woodwork. There'll be a loud cry from marketing if we cut them loose."

He pulled another sheet from the folder.

"If you look at revenue contribution breakdown, operating costs, and line-by-line profitability, a pattern begins to emerge. Those that produce the least, cost the most."

Ed peered obediently.

"So," he said, "it becomes apparent that the old 80–20 rule still applies. Eighty percent of the activities produce only 20 percent of the total results. But the division has been going through a massive exercise in streamlining and cutting fat for the past 18 months. The board has been very proud of the results you attained."

"All true," said Nick. "However, what we did was trim up the existing operation. We never looked at our basic strategy. So now we've patched up the old house and made it less expensive to run. We have a lot of family members who don't pull their own weight and a lot of new ones who are not being fed properly. That leads to a lot of dumb things like putting part of the quality department in purchasing and cutting back on preventive maintenance."

"You feel those things were motivated by managers forced to cut costs regardless of the effect? Isn't there any philosophical reason for taking such action?"

"They blush when asked about it," said Nick. "It really was a bad idea and has been reversed. I'm very disturbed that they would so casually drop something so basic in order to meet a short-term goal. We'll address that at the quarterly management meeting."

"What is Jim Andling's reaction to this plan? Have you had a chance to discuss it with him in any detail?"

Nick shrugged.

"I think Jim is going to love it. He has no patience with keeping things going just because they're traditional. My problem is with the group executive, Carson Goldman. He went into shock when I outlined it all to him. He's scared that our unbroken string of improved earnings will be tarnished, and that's all he can think about."

"Will it? Be tarnished?" asked Ed.

"It's a possibility, at least for a moment or two. I know we'll make more of everything over a 5-year period, and we should be out of sight in 10 years. But who knows about 5 years—let alone 10?"

"What is Carson's hang-up?" asked Ed.

"I think it has to do with what he considers a sudden change. Actually, I've been thinking about it for a long time but never had the guts to take it on until I joined your group. I guess the idea that both you and Jim thought I could be truly effective pushed me over the wall," said Nick.

"You never thought you were effective before?" asked Ed.

"Not really. I made a lot of things happen, but mostly it was carrying out someone else's plan. If you're halfway smart and appear confident, you can get almost anything done in the depths of a big organization. They think you know what you're doing.

"But making life-and-death decisions is another matter. There are not many facts about the future. Carson might be right, but I think he just wants a couple more years of peace and quiet and then Jim will make him president," said Nick.

"He might be underestimating Jim," said Ed. "But that's not my problem. My problem is you and what we can do to give your plan a fair shake."

"I'm all ears," said Nick.

Communicating the Need to Change

"We obviously need to get this all laid out in a way that everyone can understand, Ed continued. "It needs to be put into a presentation format with the concept, projections, and actions laid out. It doesn't have to be in great detail. That can be done by the staff groups. But the logic and the benefit have to come across strongly—and rapidly. These people have short attention spans."

"Which group of 'these people' do you mean?" asked Nick. "Jim, Carson, and the senior executives?"

"Certainly them, but they would come second in terms of actual implementation. We need to bring your team on board and give them a chance to identify any weak spots and do some preliminary planning. You're going to need to identify the crossover costs and get an idea about how much hostility all this is going to breed, if any. My guess is that they'll all want to do it."

"What about the morale problem? If we do all this up-front presentation, then there'll certainly be a leak and all the people will be upset that we're going to dump them. You know how those things happen. We need to prevent having that kind of problem," worried Nick.

"What would you suggest?" asked Ed.

"Well, there's no use getting my team involved if it's not going to get past the top management. What would you think about Jim, Carson, and me having a meeting to see if the idea is going to fly at all?" asked Nick.

"Did Carson have anything at all encouraging to say when you talked to him about it? Was there the slightest bit of redeeming value in his comment?" asked Ed.

"Not much. He did say something about always having to prepare for the future. But that was it."

"Okay. 'Preparing for the future' it is. Let's block out a few charts under that title. Then you can tell both of them that you have an idea that needs discussing. Tell Carson you're using his title and then just assume his agreement. Don't go around asking permission to do what you already are commissioned to do. But don't stomp on someone just because they happen to be in the way."

"Will you help me think it out?" asked Nick.

"I'm not going to understand all the products and market considerations you folks take for granted. However, we can develop the approach clearly by taking an example from a much smaller business. Let's take a company that has about $30 million in sales, several product lines, and a dissatisfaction with its return on investment."

"I would bet that you just happen to have one like that in your briefcase. Right?" said Nick.

"You must be a futurist," answered Ed. "Let me show you a chart on the Adams Software Company. Let's say that one of their young executives is presenting this for us to decide how to make the company more profitable. Here's the graphic."

ADAMS SOFTWARE

(In Thousands)

Revenues: $31,625   Gross Income: $3,285
Expenses: $28,340   Net Income: $1,905

Product	Revenues	Expenses	Gross
Standard software	$18,450	$15,129	$ 3,320
Special software	2,150	4,140	(1,990)
Customer training	6,785	5,225	1,560
Consulting	4,240	3,850	390

"Having shown this chart, the proposer got up and said that he would like to recommend that the company raise its special software prices and consider expanding that operation. Then he sat down. What do you suppose the reaction was?" asked Ed.

"They probably rose as one and tossed him out on his ear," smiled Nick. "But since it's you showing it to me, I can only assume that they all decided that the need was to lose more money, and they made him president of the company by acclamation—although I would have a hard time coming to that conclusion based on this evidence. I would need more."

"Exactly," said Ed. "You would want to understand the logic. Actually, in this case it turns out the standard software they sell so profitably originates with the special products they make for clients. In essence, that's their research and development laboratory. If they can learn how to price that service better, they can run it at no cost to themselves."

"What's the difference between customer training and consulting? Do the same people do both?" asked Nick.

"No, they don't. The groups are separate. The consultants cost a lot more money to have and to supply."

"If they were able to use the customer training people to do it all, they would do a lot to reduce expenses," noted Nick.

"You're really catching on to this evaluation business," said Ed. "The consultants have really been used to 'sell and troubleshoot.' But they're a lot of trouble and don't generate much on their own. So they're being phased out, and training is being expanded.

"Several of the key consultants have been formed into a strategy group that helps clients put their information systems together. That's something clients will pay for happily. The rest have gone out into the world and are doing well. Most of them use Adams products for their new employers."

"And the company is doing well?"

"Yes. By aiming their organization in the proper direction rather than just following industry practice, they've moved out strongly. Profitability has doubled. That's what I think you're planning for the electronics division."

Ed put the papers back in the briefcase.

"I have some others if you need further reassurance."

Nick held up his hand.

"I know the financial aspects are right, and I know this gives us a big jump on quality improvement. What concerns me are the relationships. I don't need to turn Carson into someone who distrusts me. He's been very helpful and positive over the years," said Nick.

"Then he will be on this matter also, as long as you don't give the impression you're trying to push him out of the way."

"I'm going to try to set up this meeting for the end of the week, and if I don't get sent down in flames, I'll bring my team together the first of next week. We'll put together an action package that'll aim us at the target.

"I really think we could implement this whole thing in a few months. The employees should feel good about it. There'll be growth and opportunity rather than continual contraction and cost cutting. The biggest problem will be selling off those product lines we don't want."

Nick was pacing around the room.

"What's the main reason companies have trouble selling off units they don't need anymore? It has to be done rapidly in order to cut down the static."

Ed nodded.

"Price, usually. The selling company wants to make money on the deal. Instead, they should just get the best they can and move along. Eliminating what is not wanted or needed is profitable in itself."

"We'll be cutting out a third of our revenues but only a couple percent of profit. We can replace the revenues quickly by expanding the component operation. The president of Bravo is going to head up all that, although he doesn't know about it yet. That case movie of yours saved us a lot of trouble. We would've lost some good people," said Nick.

"That'll probably be a good move," commented Ed. "Successful people breed success. Do you have some good backup in that area?"

"Yes. Also, we're going to make acquisitions or joint ventures in Europe and on the Pacific Rim. We're going to put this division into a really worldwide business. The only way to grow continually is to be a real part of every economy. Then you can have customers everywhere."

An Ongoing Willingness to Learn

Nick was becoming more expansive now that his confidence was restored. He smiled at Ed.

"Let me ask you a question off the record. How do I go about becoming the chief executive of this corporation or one I can make into something like this one? Do I have the talent or whatever it takes?"

Ed put his case down and leaned back in the chair.

"You have the talent, the energy, and the smarts. It takes a bit of luck also, but sometimes that comes to those who just keep shooting. There's nothing keeping you from that sort of goal except yourself and the opportunity. Both of those are manageable.

"I'm convinced that the key to a useful and satisfying life, at least the part we human beings can do something about, lies in the willingness to learn and continue learning.

"For instance, you and I have had the same education as far as the degree hanging on the office wall would tell. We both work in the same business environment, and we both know how to utilize the world we live in.

"However, when I went to college and when I entered the business world, there were no computers, no dial phones, no fax, no duplicating machines, no jet planes, no female executives, no Japanese competition, no leveraged buyouts, and a much longer list of things and systems that just didn't exist.

"Over the years I've had to learn how to understand and deal with these things. Also, I've had to learn how to understand and deal with people as they've developed. There are new customs and new requirements.

"You take computers as a matter of course. My grandchildren use them as toys. I still have to think about them each time I sit down in front of one. For me, the electric typewriter was a breakthrough invention. If there's been that much change in my lifetime, think what's going to happen by the time you're my age. We're getting behind just sitting here."

Nick nodded.

"I really hadn't thought about things that way. I've always made a point of trying to keep up, but you're saying that I have to keep *ahead* of everyone else. How would I know if I began to slip behind?"

Ed chuckled.

"It usually begins by being against whatever is proposed, particularly if it requires change. That's how so many companies got their telephone systems in bad shape. They didn't take time to understand what was involved with owning their own and such.

"At any rate, it's necessary to devote time and energy to learning ahead of everything else. When you don't want to do that anymore, it's time to negotiate early retirement while they still love you."

"I'll let you know how all this comes out," said Nick.

11
Anna

Handling a Highly Sensitive Situation

Anna Novello always began her workday with a tour of the facility, making certain that she spoke to each person. The employees viewed her trip as a courtesy. She looked at it as an audit. Her department heads hated every moment of it. When Anna returned to her office, she had a list of inadequacies for them to do something about. And for Anna, "do something about" meant right now.

"She is the sweetest thing I've ever seen," said Alice Gordon. "I've worked for Alabank as a teller for 22 years now, and Anna is the best manager I've ever had. She's thoughtful and considerate, she never raises her voice, and she's willing to step right in and help without even being asked. She was a teller once, you know."

"She's a tigress," said Alfred Whaps. "Just between us, she's as tough as nails under that velvet exterior. She thinks only of herself and her career. She does whatever it takes to get people to work hard. If that means being nice, then she's nice. If it means busting chops, then she busts chops. I don't know which is the real Anna."

An Unexpected Byproduct of Paying Attention

Ed and Anna began their session together at a fast-food restaurant. While Ed was digging through a bowl of chili, Anna picked at a salad. This was their first session since the community discussion. Ed always felt you could get to know someone better in a fast-food place than in a white-tablecloth establishment. Somehow there was less pretension involved.

"I've been wanting to ask you, Ed," she said, "what you think the biggest problem of leadership is. Why are there so few good leaders and why do so many people fail when it appears obvious that they have the capability of becoming successful?"

"If I answer that, we'll be here till dinner time. However, let me take a crack at it.

"Once I went to a seminar conducted by a well-known writer. He had produced hundreds of articles and a dozen books, all of them successful. He did this seminar for a token fee because he felt an obligation to help others learn the craft. The first subject the students brought up, he told me— and it was the same with every group—was 'Where do I get an agent?' and questions about other business aspects of writing.

"His comment was always the same. 'Writers write,' he would say. 'When you write something the world wants, it will get published. First write, then get agents and the other stuff.'

"So, although I charge a lot more for my advice than he does, it is essentially the same. Leaders lead; others pretend to lead. To lead you have to be concentrated, or focused, on something that you want to happen. And the leader has to get the message across to those who will carry it out.

"For instance, the big management thrust today is for consensus. Executives bring their people together and go through extensive exercises to bring forth an agreed-upon strategy. This is done with the thought that something developed in this manner will be supported and executed enthusiastically by the team. Unfortunately, what emerges is usually a compromise and may not represent the best thinking or even the most effective way of doing things. The process of arriving at consensus can develop peace and quiet, but it rarely produces innovation and excitement. Such things usually originate with an individual.

"Consensus should be used for implementation but not for determination. The executive needs to determine what must be done, using all the resources available. Then the team is brought together to refine the concept and figure how to implement it. The team will be happy with this opportunity to contribute and will develop a plan they can all support. It is not the doing that creates division; it is the conceiving of what to do."

"I can see the logic of that, and I have to admit that most of the good things I've seen in management have come from one person. Groups or committees seem to be able to refine or improve on them though," Anna commented.

"Very true. It's the original idea that groups have a difficult time generating. The whole concept of branch banking, for instance, came out of one person's head. The implementation has been the result of a lot of effort by a lot of people. Most of the financial instruments we deal with are individual creations, but their uses certainly aren't." Ed returned to his chili.

"Speaking of financial instruments, there's something that's been bothering me, and I haven't been able to discuss it with anyone. It's a matter that involves the whole bank, not just my branch. Do you think it would be proper for you and me to discuss it?" asked Anna.

Ed hesitated.

"I'm not supposed to get into operating topics. We're concentrating on your personal development as an executive. One part of that development is learning how to deal with sensitive items. So it's your call. Whatever you tell me remains between us, and my job is to give you an honest answer—when I know the answer."

Ed smiled at her as she struggled with the decision. When she looked up at him, he could see there was real worry in her eyes. She looked younger than her years at that moment.

"I think one, or several, of the bank's senior officers are stealing from the bank," she said. "And I just don't know what to do about it."

Ed was shaken.

"That wasn't exactly the kind of problem I had anticipated," he said. "Why don't we hold this part of our conversation until we get back in the car?"

They finished lunch in silence and moved quietly out to the automobile. Ed drove a few blocks to a parking lot beside a lake. He stopped the car, opened the windows, and they sat for a moment as the silence continued.

"Does Betty know about this?" he asked.

She shook her head.

"I haven't told a soul. I'm not sure who's involved and who isn't. I don't know what to do with my information. I do feel that I should talk with Betty or someone before going to the police or the banking commission or whomever one goes to."

Ed nodded.

"Probably the FBI," he said. "They know everyone who would want to know. Well, before we get too carried away, why don't you take me through the whole story so I can understand what makes you think this way. Don't bother editing it as you go. I'll take care of that."

Anna smiled a little bit and then began. She was regaining her confidence.

"Well, as you know, one of my personal behavior problems is that I have to see if each system we use is the most efficient it can be. I'm always getting static about changing the way we sort mail, or count the cash, or run personnel, or something. I guess if I were a homemaker, I'd be trying out new table settings every meal.

"Several months ago I started fiddling with the wire-transfer system in the branch. We have a lot of business accounts. We have one company paying another company for

services, writing a check on their account. They mail the
check to the supplier, who writes across the back and sends it
back to us to deposit in their account. I figured we could do
the whole thing by wire transfer. That way people could get
paid the same day they send an invoice. It would cut down on
their accounts receivables."

Ed was listening carefully.

"I thought companies liked to wait as along as possible before paying in order to collect interest on the money," he
said.

"I was able to show them that the cost of clerks and handling during that period amounted to a lot more than the interest they were gaining. It drops the hassle down to nothing.
But they do it because they receive more than they send out
and get it quicker than they did before.

"Anyway," she continued, "that started to work out so well
that I began to look into the money-market and certificate-
of-deposit accounts we carry. When interest matures in any
of them, we have to notify the client, who can take it out or
roll it over. A lot of them take it out since it's a main part of
their income.

"A great deal of paperwork is involved here, too. By using
some of the wire transfer knowledge we gained and by letting people make assignments in advance, we've been able to
cut a lot of costs out of this system. A wire transfer costs
about 30 cents. The check writing, mailing, and clearing is
closer to three dollars. And the clients on both ends of the
wire are happier too."

When she stopped for a breath, Ed urged her on. He was
waiting for the punch line.

"All of that work puts you in areas that are not normally
seen by a branch manager, I imagine," he encouraged.

She glanced sharply at him.

"True," she said, "and most enlightening. After my first
three or four examinations of the computer files, I found
that there were a couple of wire-transfer accounts blocked
out."

"'Blocked out'?" repeated Ed.

"That means they were not available to anyone who didn't have a specific code number. These are all computer programs, and they can be guarded."

"Isn't that a common situation? I mean aren't most of the accounts protected?" he asked.

"You have to identify yourself and use your entrance number, but all the regular transfer accounts are accessible to officers. Many trust or private accounts can't be reached except by certain people. But when you call up the account, the computer tells you who that is, and you can go ask. These accounts just sit there. They don't respond to any prodding. However, the access request number on the file does note that someone asked."

She was becoming excited.

"These have a different level of secrecy?" asked Ed.

"They are original, and no one would ever know they are around because they are buried in the reserved account numbers for wire transfer."

"What do these accounts do? Do you know?"

She nodded.

"I've figured it out, I think. It's really an ingenious plan. We were talking about original work. *This* is an original.

"What's happening is that the money-market funds are being shorted by a tenth of a percent on an annual basis. This means that every thousand dollars comes out to be $999. The other dollar goes into this account. It could be covered as being a transfer charge or something. No one is going to make a fuss even if they notice it."

"I don't know how much money Alabank manages in money markets," said Ed, "but I'm sure it's a bunch."

"How does two billion dollars grab you?" asked Anna. "If you do the mathematics on that, it comes out to $2,000,000 each and every year for our mystery account. The money disappears into the wire-transfer system and whisks off into the night. I'm not sure where it whisks off to."

"Probably somewhere in the Caribbean," said Ed. "There are a lot of banks throughout the islands that like to do business with quiet accounts. How long do you think this has been going on?"

She shrugged.

"I have no way of knowing. The numbers are old ones on the account list, so I suspect it's been some time."

"When did Alabank begin to have money-market funds?" he asked. "That's only been six or seven years, hasn't it?"

"When Allison Gilbert joined the bank. She came from New York and was hired for that purpose. I think that's been seven years. It's been a very successful program, and Allison is slated to succeed Betty when she retires in three years," Anna replied.

There was a long pause.

"Have you thought about who's doing this?" asked Ed.

"I've thought about little else for the past two weeks," said Anna. "There are a few obvious suspects, but I do think it has to be a senior executive or maybe a group of them. It's just too hard for lower-level or junior people to get much access to real money in a bank. Most of the employee embezzlements involve petty cash or tapping a dormant account. This thing is well organized and has been going on for a long time.

"Well, doctor," she said, "what do I do now?"

"What do you think you should do?" asked Ed.

"It's a puzzle. My impulse is to go see Betty, but I'm afraid she'll just think I'm trying to discredit Allison. And even if she doesn't, she'll feel that those who could be involved will deserve the chance to offer an explanation. I know she doesn't have much understanding of computers. The culprits could wipe out all the evidence in 10 minutes at a personal computer."

"Isn't there any way of making a record of what's on the computer now?" asked Ed. "Then no matter what happens, there'll at least be some evidence."

Anna reached into her purse and pulled out a small disc.

"It's all on here," she said. "I suppose they could say I made it up."

"Not likely," said Ed. "Put that in a safety deposit box in

another bank. We'll go find one right now. And then I think you and I should go see Betty. She's a lot smarter than you might think on people relationships. Then we'll notify the FBI and let them take it from there."

He turned to look at Anna.

"You'll be placed in a difficult position when this all hits the streets. How it all comes out depends on the way you handle yourself with media and bank people. You're just a bank officer who discovered a defalcation while doing a routine part of your job. Be careful to avoid giving the impression that you were poking around the bank records playing detective, which you weren't."

Reporting the Unpleasant Truth

They stopped by the bank where Anna's cousin worked and rented a safety deposit box. Anna carried Ed's briefcase with her to give the impression that she had a lot of documents to drop off. But as they left, the only thing lying in the box was a small black disc.

Betty was pleased to see Anna and Ed.

"The professor and the student," she smiled. "It's good to see both of you. I hear great things about your school system, Ed. Jim Andling tells me that Nick is completely transforming Marlot."

"Well, one division at least," replied Ed.

Ed nodded to Anna, who was nervous about this whole thing. She smiled at Betty and began.

"I asked Ed to come with me, Betty, because I have something very difficult and important to say. He's providing moral support and is not part of the situation."

Betty was concerned.

"What is it?" she asked. "You can tell me anything; you know that."

"Oh, I know that, Betty, and I feel comfortable with you. But you'll see why I wanted to be careful."

"Okay. What's this 'situation'? Just tell me," Betty said.

"Someone is drawing two million dollars a year out of our money-market funds and putting it away for their own use. This may have been going on for several years."

Betty's face showed her shock.

"How did you find out about this?" she inquired sharply.

"I was trying to find a better system of using wire transfers to move interest to customers' checking accounts. I noticed that the same account number appeared every time a new deposit, interest payment, or withdrawal was made. I just came across it because the dollar amount being moved was always one-tenth of 1 percent of the value involved. We have over two billion dollars being invested; that produces around two million dollars a year that someone is skimming."

Betty was thinking.

"Does Allison know about this?" she asked, reaching for the telephone.

"Just the three of us know," said Anna. "I might suggest that we keep it to this group, at least until we've talked with the FBI."

Betty hung up the phone and gazed at Anna.

"I think that might be good advice. But before we call anyone, I'd like to see some evidence on this. Is there anything you can show me?"

Anna stood up.

"If I may use your computer terminal for a few moments, I think it may be possible to dig something up."

The women exchanged seats, and Betty turned to Ed as Anna began to work on the computer.

"I have to admit that I've never been comfortable with these machines. Now we see that our pockets can be picked electronically, and we'd never know it.

"Do you think all this is true, Ed? I find it hard to believe that one of our people would do something like this."

Ed frowned.

"You never know about people and stealing. But it's hard to understand why anyone would do such a thing," he said. "However, it usually isn't for the money. It's for some other reason: pride, showing off, revenge, to achieve some short-range goal. Who knows? But whoever's doing this one is pretty smart about it."

"Not smart enough to quit in time," said Betty.

In a short while, Anna had called up the necessary systems and was able to show Betty the accounts in question.

"I can't go any further without the entry code," said Anna.

"Just a minute," said Betty.

She went over to the small safe in her bookcase and returned with an undersized, three-ring binder. After looking through the contents sheet, she turned to the page she was wanting.

"We have a computer security system that keeps track of all codes as well as many other things. This book is the only file with everything in it. If there's an access code, it's in here. If it isn't in here, then we have a much bigger problem that you've brought me."

Anna searched the page and the computer file for the next 15 minutes.

"This might be it," she said as she punched the numbers on the keys. All three of them peered at the screen, which suddenly displayed a whole information sheet.

"These are withdrawal figures on a daily basis for the past two months," said Anna. "It shows that one-tenth of 1 percent of any new money is lifted right out."

"If you did it on the whole account each day, the box would be empty before long. Tapping new deposits makes it look like a fee, if anyone would ever notice," said Ed.

Betty was beginning to become angry and was obviously hurt. But she recovered herself immediately.

"This is a despicable act. I think the thing to do is notify the FBI right now. We have to keep this quiet in the bank until they tell us what to do."

She pulled the phone book out of her credenza, looked up the number, and placed the call herself.

When the conversation ended, she turned to face Anna and Ed.

"Anna, you have a lot of courage and sense. You may have

saved the bank a great deal of trouble, and you may have caused a great deal of trouble. We'll have to see. But you did the right thing, and the fact that you were working so hard to improve something when you discovered it speaks well for you also."

Suspicion Confirmed

"The FBI agents will be here in 30 minutes. Why don't the three of us relax and have a cup of coffee?"

As they seated themselves, the secretary's voice came over the intercom.

"Ms. Gilbert is on the line. She's very anxious to speak with you. Should I have her call back?"

Betty glanced at the others.

"I'll take it, Helen. Put it on the conference-table phone."

She sat down and answered, then listened for a few moments.

"Why don't you come over to my office right now, Allison?" she said. "Anna is here with Ed Kargston. They'll be interested in what you have to say. See you in a minute."

Betty hung up the phone and turned to her guests.

"Allison says that there's a computer hacker trying to work in our system. I suspect they're discovering the investigation you've been doing, Anna. The computer room just picked up that someone was accessing classified information. Can they do that?"

"They would have to be lucky," replied Anna. "We have dozens of terminals accessing information from the same mainframe all the time. It would be interesting to know how this was identified. The MIS [Management Information Systems] people could tell us, I'm sure."

Just then Allison entered. A tall, attractive woman, she was obviously upset by the news she was carrying. She responded automatically to Ed as she was introduced and nodded to Anna. She obviously was hesitant about sharing her news with these people.

"It's all right, Allison," said Betty, "Anna and Ed are interested in hearing about this hacker, too."

"Well, it's very sensitive. We could be in a lot of trouble if someone from the outside has our codes. They can jiggle our accounts around, take money anytime they want, and even put themselves on the payroll. We're going to have to change everything."

Betty motioned for her to sit down.

"How did you find that someone was tapping into your data systems? Does a bell go off or something?" asked Ed.

Allison glanced quickly at him and then began to relax a little.

"No, there isn't any bell. But there are some signs. Someone used to working an account will notice a small change in it that can't be explained. It's like coming home and realizing that something's not exactly where you put it."

"Who realized that?" asked Anna.

"Huh?" said Allison.

"What person realized that someone had been eating their porridge? Was it an individual, or is the whole MIS group involved?"

"Actually," said Allison, "it was Walter Jamison, the MIS manager, who mentioned it to me. He had been talking with Winnie Hector."

"Who's Winnie Hector?" asked Ed.

"Our number two in finance," said Betty. "Winnie's been at Alabank for 10 years. She's very dedicated to the organization. We're very proud of her. She was elected the state's Service Woman of the Year this past January. Her family is well known. They've been here forever. Winnie has never married and is independently wealthy. She's interested in every charity going."

Ed and Anna stopped breathing. Allison stared at them.

"What is it with you two?" she asked. "You both look like you're ready to pop. Did I say something wrong?"

"No, Allison," replied Ed. "I think you may have started things on the right path."

"Let me fill you in on what we've learned, or think we've learned," said Betty. "Apparently, someone is using the computer to tap the money-market system for about two million dollars a year."

Allison stood up quickly and gasped.

"No! That just can't be. We monitor those funds continually. No one could possibly touch any of it. We have the most effective security system in the nation, in the world for that matter."

She was pale.

Betty put her arm around Allison to calm her.

"Take it easy, easy. If something is happening, it's because of technology, not controls. I know you've done everything possible. The FBI will be here in a few minutes, and we'll let them handle it. No one will blame you or your system."

Allison sat down but didn't seem convinced that everything was going to be satisfactory.

The FBI people came, and working in conjunction with the bank examiners and Alabank's MIS staff, soon determined that Anna's suspicions were correct. Better than eight million dollars had been taken over a four-year period. As Ed had suspected, Winnie Hector was the architect of the defalcation. She confessed as soon as she was asked. In fact, she had been stealing for all of the 10 years she had worked at Alabank. Her family fortune had disappeared, and she hated to disappoint the charitable organizations they had contributed to over the years.

Aftermath: Back to Basics

A few weeks later, Ed and Anna resumed their session.

"She gave it all away," said Anna. "I'm sure in her mind that it was not an improper thing to do."

"Well, she's headed for state prison now," commented Ed. "She'll never have the opportunity to get near anyone's bank account again."

"I appreciate your help in all this, Ed," said Anna. "But I'm afraid it didn't have much to do with learning to be an executive. What do I need to do more of?"

"You're a rare combination of characteristics, Anna," said Ed. "You're a natural leader, but you also like to take things into your own hands, and you learn from doing so. Your natural curiosity leads you into many areas. We need to work on changing the way you impact people. It's easy to assume that someone is criticizing when really they're trying to bring about improvement.

"The way you handled this embezzlement was a good example of what you can do when you consider the situation to be serious. You took very sure steps, and no one became upset or felt threatened by what you were doing. In fact, a great deal of positive reaction and credit came your way.

"However, something like the mail-sorting and distribution system didn't receive the same kind of thought, at least when it came to relationships. The branch has a more effective system than any other area, but no one likes it. We need to get that straight before you move to your new job in headquarters."

"I was very pleased that Allison recommended that job for me. Betty was hesitant to do it, I know. She didn't want everyone to come to the conclusion that she was pushing me along," said Anna.

"Remember, there are three aspects to the executive's life—" said Ed, "finance, quality, and relationships. Most of the work you've been doing could be considered quality, making things come out right every time. You need more work on relationships, as we've been discussing. But how about finance? Does your branch make money? If so, why? If not, why not? What sort of measures, controls, and improvement programs do you have?"

Anna thought about this for a moment.

"It's interesting that you bring this up. I've been thinking about those questions myself, and I have to say that I have no answers. We get very little measurement data here. Everything is set up from downtown. I get to negotiate the people budget, but that's not hard to do once a person becomes familiar with the work load in a branch. So we fight every quarter about clerks and such. But I have no idea if the outfit is making money on its transactions. I wonder if anyone else does?

"That sounds like a good subject for my next investigation. If I can determine what information is available now, then I'll know what I need." She was excited about it.

"You might think about it the other way around," suggested Ed. "What do you need to determine how things are doing on a regular basis? What data are required? Just make a list right now."

Anna was startled.

"But I don't know much about accounting, although I plan to take some courses in it next fall. I'm not even familiar with the words."

Ed shook his head.

"It isn't that complicated. But you have to know something about all the actions it takes to run a business. Betty, for instance, has never been able to work the computer capabilities into her management style. It's always an add-on, and she admits it. But it becomes a weakness. Actually, there's nothing a computer can do that can't be done by hand. The difference is time and capacity. Not everyone understands that.

"Now let's take your personal finances. Do you know how much money you're taking in?"

Anna nodded.

"Do you know where it comes from?"

Another nod.

"Do you know your obligations?"

"And I know my expenses on top of that. I do well with my personal finances. Of course, I never have any left over, and I have very little in my savings account. But input and outputs I do okay," Anna stated.

"Good," said Ed. "Now let's apply the same thought process to the branch. Where does the income originate?"

"Well," said Anna, "it comes from interest paid by customers on their loans, primarily; also from checking account fees and other service fees such as traveler's checks. We also receive closing fees on mortgages, but most of those are done downtown."

"Okay," nodded Ed, "now we know enough to begin laying out the revenue stream. A chat with the comptroller will tell you about any other items. But you'll want to keep track of each of these components on a real-time basis. It isn't enough to look at it once a month. Streams flow, and they can change courses quickly."

"All I have to do is find the data source and program the information into my computer. Then I can use graphics and hook up to real time. If there's some change I need to know about, it's no trouble to make a hard copy," said Anna.

"I can do the same with expenses. However, as I think about it, I suspect my figures will show a loss if we do honest reporting and include rent and other overhead. The bank figures are on the overall corporation. It would probably be more efficient if we had fewer branches."

"The reason there are so many branches," said Ed, "is that some years ago it was learned that every branch attracts so many deposits and then seems to flatten out. Theoretically, you could put one on each of the four corners in this intersection and they would all grow the same. Of course, customer service and traffic patterns fit into it, too."

"You mean that a lot of bank executives think anyone can run a branch? I've long suspected that," snapped Anna.

"I didn't mean that or say that. However, that might be a pattern in some circles. If you were a 55-year-old veteran branch manager, male, and saw yourself being outdistanced by a 31-year-old female, you might be tempted to make up stories like that."

Ed smiled at her.

"Well, you go to work on the finance comprehension area, and we'll chat again in a couple of weeks. In the meantime, begin laying out your early plan for taking over this new job. You'll need at least to have an idea of what's going to be involved. Have you talked much with Allison about it?"

"No, I really haven't had time yet," she admitted.

"Back to relationships. You need to make time and fit into her schedule. It's necessary to understand what she's expecting so you can plan accordingly. Then you can meet her expectations or get them changed if they don't fit the need. But now's the time to build a relationship. Don't wait until you're both buried in anthills and covered with maple syrup."

12
Harold

Overseeing a Major Corporate Overhaul

"Financing leases or just lending money to businesses is the way to go, Ed," said Harold. "The people borrowing take it all very seriously, but deep in their hearts they know that they personally don't have to pay it back. Financing instead of paying for it in cold, hard cash leaves liquid assets on the balance sheet. That makes everyone look good and feel comfortable.

"They buy our bonds, which are usually pegged to pay a point or two below prime, and borrow the money at a point or two above prime. It's the same money."

Ed shifted in his seat and waited for Harold to finish his discussion. Harold, noticing that he was losing his audience, looked at Ed expectantly.

"Well, what should we get into, Ed?" he asked. "I didn't make an agenda or any plans. So whatever fits with your schedule is perfect with me."

"What would you have been doing today if I weren't here?" asked Ed.

Harold smiled.

"I would have been having a bunch of meetings with people who were trying to sell me on projects or trying to get special interest rates for some customer. It's like that every day," said Harold.

"Is that the way you like it?" asked Ed.

"Not necessarily, but it kind of has to be that way. Mr. Smith expects his top people to know everything that goes on, and the only way *that* can happen is if we're *involved* in everything that goes on. I must say, though, that it seems to me to be a good way of working. We never have any surprises. And he hates surprises," noted Harold.

"But this is a very big division of a very big company," said Ed. "How can you develop people if they have to bring everything through the top of the bottle? Don't they get a little frustrated?" asked Ed.

"We like to think that they appreciate the opportunity to become involved in decision making. They get an exposure that wouldn't be available to them in other companies," said Harold.

"Exposure?" asked Ed.

"Yes, they get to sit with senior executives while the subject is being discussed, put in their comments, and then hear the decision firsthand. It's sort of a broader version of what you're doing," smiled Harold.

"I wonder if they view it that way," mused Ed. "I would think they might feel the system was rather unstructured."

"Well, there's a way to settle it," said Harold. "Let's just open the faucets and see who shows up with what pieces of paper and what projects. Let me tell Jim what we're going to do."

"Spare the Rod and Spoil the Employee"

While Harold disappeared for a few moments, Ed poured himself another cup of coffee and nibbled absently at a muffin. He hated it when there was food around to eat while he killed time. If it wasn't there, he wouldn't be tempted; and he didn't really want the stuff anyway. It was just something to do.

Harold returned with two people in tow.

"Ed Kargston, this is Hilary Wilson and this is Tom Rachel. Hilary is from the Chicago office. Tom works for the MIS headquarters group. Both of them have what we call PARs or Proposal Action Requests. I don't know where we got that name. It doesn't make a lot of sense."

"Everyone knows that it means someone wants money and has to go fight for it. They're commonly called "poor and 'retched'" because they're sad to behold after management gets through with them," said Tom.

"I don't know that we want to bore Ed with our internal gossip, Tom," said Harold testily. "Hilary, do you want to explain your PAR?"

Hilary nervously handed both men copies of the request.

"This involves a new reception area for the downtown Chicago office. The whole building is being dressed up and the owners have asked us to participate by upgrading our entrance and reception area. It does look pretty bad. The PAR is for $2500 this year and $14,000 during the first quarter of next year." She smiled hopefully.

"Is the owner going to reduce our rent by this amount?" asked Harold.

Hilary blushed.

"We didn't discuss that, Mr. Clark," she replied. "I assume the owner figures that since they're spending a couple million dollars on the improvement, the tenants would do their share."

"So we never would get any return on our money, right?" stated Harold, his eyes on the paper.

Hilary stammered.

"No, I guess not. Actually, as I said, the place does look pretty bad now, and we would have to do something sooner or later. The executive committee thought we should go ahead with it," she replied.

There was a brief silence.

"Should I take it back?" asked Hilary.

Harold glanced at her.

"Actually, Hilary, I'm surprised that it was even sent down. The building is the landlord's problem. I realize that this is a relatively small amount of money, but I don't think we want to set a precedent with this case. We have dozens of offices around the country. If you multiply them by that amount, it suddenly becomes a large amount.

"So I'll mark disapproved on here, and you take it back. Perhaps they can think of another way of dressing up the front office."

He handed her the paper and took the one Tom had laid on the table. As he studied it, Hilary just sat there and Tom hesitantly began to describe the proposal.

"We have to go to laser printers in the MIS system. The old ones are too slow. We can phase them out over a period of time, but it's going to cost about $650,000 over the next seven months. The productivity gains should more than pay for it."

Harold nodded and scribbled his initials on the upper right-hand corner.

"We have to keep ahead of progress, I guess, Tom," He looked up at the younger people.

"Okay," he said. "If that's all then, we'll let you both get back to work. Hilary, thank you so much for coming down from Chicago. I'll look for you the next time I'm in that office."

They shook hands and left.

Harold turned to Ed.

"Bright young people," he said.

"I wouldn't worry about saying hello to her in the Chicago office, Harold," said Ed. "She isn't going to be there much longer."

Harold was startled.

"How can you know that? She's only been with us for a few months. In fact, this is her first trip to headquarters. As a matter of fact, we went to a great deal of trouble to recruit her. She graduated in the upper 3 percent of her MBA class, and we have a great future in mind for her. Why should she leave?"

It was Ed's turn to be startled.

"Let me ask you, Harold. Suppose you went to see the big boss to ask if it was all right to get a drink of water from the cooler and were told that it couldn't be afforded. And while you were waiting, someone came and asked if they could go to the Four Seasons for lunch on the company and that was granted. Would you feel like working there?"

"I really don't understand what you're saying, Ed. You'll have to make it clearer for me."

"Are you really not aware that you humiliated that young lady, that you treated her like some kind of nitwit who brought a stupid proposal all the way from Chicago? And then after turning her down, you agreed to buy enough new printers to pave the highway to Chicago without even knowing much about them? Weren't you listening to yourself?"

Ed was becoming upset.

"You don't understand Eastland, Ed," said Harold. "That's the way our people learn. Sure, I was a little difficult with her, but she'll look at those PARs much closer in the future. It was good for her."

"She has no future here, Harold. You'll see. And if you don't want to wait and see, let's call up the human resources director and ask what the turnover rate is for the new MBAs you all recruit so effectively. How long do they stay, and how many of those who stay have been promoted to management-level jobs?" Ed suggested.

"Are you saying that we chase them away by not being soft on them? I really don't see what you're getting at. Mr. Smith set that pattern in the company years ago, and we've all learned that it's effective," said Harold.

"This company has a long-standing reputation for not growing executives. The headhunters never go after the top people at Eastland. But they like the entry-level people. You do a good job of hiring," noted Ed. "But let's check. Do you mind calling human resources?"

Harriet Wonders, the vice president of Eastland's corporate human resources operation, was not delighted at being summoned so quickly by a division president to discuss the company's innermost secrets with a stranger. However, after being reassured and coaxed, she recited some figures from memory.

"About 60 percent of the MBAs leave in the first six months, another 20 percent after a year. The others stay on and become useful members of our society. Throughout this particular division we have a turnover rate of around 20 percent a year from the weekly paid people and 9 percent from salary. The corporation as a whole does a little better: 12 percent weekly and 6 percent salary. With our strong culture, these are not unreasonable figures."

"What culture is that?" asked Ed.

They both looked at him.

"Why the Eastland culture is well known: strong interaction between executives and employees, concern for the customer, and development of a family feeling. Those are the main recognized characteristics," said Harriet.

"Do you agree, Harold?" asked Ed.

Harold beamed.

"I sure do, and there's more where those came from. We're very proud of our culture," he nodded in affirmation.

Trouble in Paradise

Ed sat back and looked at them and then shook his head.

"I tell you what I'll do. I have my checkbook here in this briefcase. I'll write a personal check for $1000 to each of your favorite charities if you can produce for me two employees under the officer level who can recite those three culture characteristics. And I'll give you another one if you can find someone who knows enough about the corporation to make a five-minute talk about it."

Ed reached in the case and removed the checkbook.

"Any takers?" he challenged.

"Are you saying we don't know our own culture?" asked Harold. "I think that might be beyond your experience, Ed. You don't know the company that well."

Harriet nodded her agreement.

"I don't know what evidence you have, Mr. Kargston, and I don't really know what your interest is, but you can be assured that this is a cohesive company."

"Do you have an orientation program—one where people are informed about the company and about those cultural characteristics?" asked Ed.

"Not a formal one," said Harriet. "But the managers in each area are expected, as part of their jobs, to bring the employees up to speed when they come aboard."

"Yes," said Harold. "We feel the best place to learn is on the job so they can get the real-life feel of the operation."

"So where," asked Ed, "do they learn about all these wonderful aspects of company life. What bonds them into a family? I've had two different experiences with Eastland and haven't seen anything indicating that the management does anything to communicate with the employees or that the employees do anything to make the company successful."

"That's a hard accusation," said Harold.

"You people are kidding yourselves, like a lot of companies do. You're careful about selecting people; but once they join, you pay absolutely no attention to them. I don't know how you expect them to learn what you think is important."

He leaned forward and asked, "Do you have a performance appraisal program? Do people get regular reviews?"

"Wallace's view always has been that those who do a good job get to keep it. But we're beginning to do regular reviews on an annual basis, as part of the merit raise system," said Harriet.

"Well, it isn't a good idea to tie those together; but it's at least a start."

He turned to Harold.

"You asked me earlier about where we should begin. I would suggest that it might be here, building a culture at Eastland," said Ed.

"That would be quite a job but well worth the effort," said Harriet.

"Would you help?" asked Harold.

"Certainly," said Harriet. "This is something I've wanted to get done for years."

"Really?" said Harold. "I never knew that. What stopped you? Don't tell me. Perhaps I don't want to know. But I think Ed's right, and I don't know why it never dawned on me before. How can people know all these things if we never tell them? Okay, let's talk."

"This is a good opportunity to consider the role of the executive," said Ed. "Here we have a corporation that thinks it has an identifiable culture but, in fact, has done nothing to make it happen. This is a typical situation where an organization was begun by one person or a family and has been managed or influenced essentially by that group. When it all started and in the early years, the culture was present and obvious. As the company grew and layers of management developed, the culture was lost except in the minds of those who 'knew it when.' They see what they want to see and imagine what they want to imagine. It wouldn't occur to them to work at establishing it.

"Of course, this is only one scenario, but it happens over and over. Some of the largest—and smallest—companies go through this. Most of them don't survive because they have a great deal of difficulty changing when it becomes necessary. In fact, they have trouble recognizing the need for change," finished Ed.

"Why do smart companies get into situations like this? Why don't they know what's happening?" asked Harriet.

"Because the executives become so sure that their system and business are well established that they don't see the need to initiate change. The managers just keep steering the ship along the same old course, never noticing that other craft are passing them in the night. It's a special kind of arrogance. I can think of 10 big companies and a dozen small ones that are heading for the reefs at this moment, full steam ahead."

Harold cocked his head.

"Do you consider Eastland one of those?" he asked.

"That's not my assignment. However, I would point out that this company has a very high turnover rate, that the earnings are flat while revenues are slipping a little bit, and that there's no clear succession of power, which is well documented in every issue of every business magazine and certainly is no secret," Ed summarized.

"When we got together the first time in the group, you talked about a company's environment. Do you consider the culture and environment the same thing? Or is one part of the other?" Harold asked.

"The working environment is everything. The culture is part of it. A culture can be overcome and drowned by a negative environment. Productivity, both blue- and white-collar, can be turned to rust. Look at the great nations that have decayed while still keeping their manners and customs. 'Genteelly shabby' is a phrase I heard once," said Ed. "It brings the thought of someone wearing proper but worn-out clothes, eating from chipped china, and discussing topics that are completely outdated and useless."

Harriet smiled.

"I never thought of it that way, but I know places like that. What a horrible thought, to go through life out of step."

"Outfits used to be able to get away with that, Harriet," said Ed. "But now they get eaten up quickly. One day they look up and the product that was the main structure of their business has been bypassed. They have to scramble around and try to catch up. They used to lead—that's almost always a characteristic—but now they follow. And that takes a different style of leadership."

"Ed," offered Harold, "I think we should spend more time on this, and I don't want to hold Harriet up any longer. My thought is that I need to pull together a team to address and attack this. Harriet will be on it, of course. Who else would you recommend?"

"Only four or five people—public relations, if they're competent—and some executives or managers that you feel are interested in the long-term success of the corporation. We could go over the list," answered Ed.

Harriet excused herself and after a few moments Harold turned to Ed and said, "I think we're going to have to have a chat with Wallace before going much further."

"Are you sure you mean 'we'?" asked Ed. "I'll be glad to go along, but it's really your show."

"Would you meet with me now and then as we go through this? I guess you're right about bearding Wallace in his den by myself. But I've been thinking about this sort of thing for some time. We're really drifting as a company, and our main product and service lines are beginning to slip. If we weren't lending money, we'd be in real trouble. And I'm not certain how long that's going to continue. The investment bankers are after our main clients."

"Tell me what you want the company to look like before you go see Wallace. You're going to have to be clear about your objectives, and he may want to know just how you plan to make these changes," Ed cautioned.

"Well, that's the problem. We're going to have to go to our people and conduct education programs that explain our theme and their role in it. And we're going to have to teach our management to manage instead of just playing traffic cop. And we're going to have to restructure the company in order to use our assets and people to the best advantage. We don't do that now," replied Harold.

"That may be where the wheels come off," he continued. "Wallace is a big part of the problem. I think he knows it, but it'll shock him if I bring it up. How do I handle that?"

Ed smiled.

"Like they say, porcupines make love 'very carefully.' But don't forget that Wallace likes you and has respect for you. He'll listen, at least for the first five minutes. I wouldn't worry about that. Go when you're ready. I'll get out of your hair now."

The men parted at the elevator, and Harold returned to his office. On the way he met Hilary, who was heading back to Chicago. She noticed him but averted her eyes.

"Hi, Hilary," he said, smiling. "I've been thinking about your office area. Do you still have the PAR?"

He reached out his hand as she pulled the document from her pouch. Taking his pen, he wrote "approved" on the front page and handed it back to her.

"You put together a good proposal, and I didn't give it proper attention. I apologize for that. Can you tell me why it's necessary to send something in this amount all the way down here? Is it in a procedure?" he asked.

"Very much in a procedure. Would you like a copy of it?" She was a little dazed but managed a smile.

"No," he said. "I probably have it in one of those books on my credenza. Why don't you write me a procedure that lays things out the way they should be. Send it to my office, and we'll issue it systemwide." He touched her on the shoulder, wished her a good trip, and went on to his office.

Changing the Corporate Culture

A few days later Harold went to meet with Wallace Smith. The chairman's office was on the top floor and accommodated personal desk space as well as a large conference table. In the far corner of the room was a comfortable seating area, and it was there that Wallace sat down with the uncomfortable Harold.

Smith rarely spoke first anymore unless he had called the meeting. He was still very much on top of things and called his executives on a daily basis. He stared quizzically at Harold and waited for some indication of what all this was about.

"I've been thinking about our growth and our earnings and have come to the conclusion that we're going to have to define and clarify our corporate culture," Harold began. "We need to give our people an identity both from the individual standpoint and from a company posture. We need to go to work on quality with a vengeance, and we need to train our executives in relationships with the employees."

"You know how to do all that, Harold?" asked Smith.

"Yes sir, I think I do," he replied. "And also we're going to have to get rid of a few businesses and bring in some other ones. The world is changing, and we're not changing with it. Frankly, sir, the company is slowing down and losing its vitality."

"You know how to do all that, Harold?" asked Smith.

Harold opened his folder.

"Here's the plan I've worked out," he offered.

Wallace took the folder and looked through the three pages inside. Accustomed to reading such things quickly, he thumbed through it twice and laid it beside his place on the table.

"This sounds like just what I've been waiting for, Harold. This will work, but not with our current management team. We'll have to move a few people out and around. Do you have a list of executive changes that need to be made?" asked the chairman.

"Not really, but I know who will have to change their ways and who will be able to handle this environment. We have some great people here at Eastland, Wallace," replied Harold. "There won't have to be many alterations."

"Well, I know one change that will have to be made. We have to get me out of the circuit," said Wallace. "I've been hoping for the past five years that someone would come in here and tell me it was time to leave because the company had to become different. And here you are."

Harold started to stammer.

"I didn't mean anything like that, sir. I was just going to point out that we've always thought we had a culture and were leading the field, but it turns out we're not," he said.

"It's going to take new hands on the tiller, Harold. I've made up my own organizational chart and will present it to the next board meeting, which happens to be day after tomorrow. It had no names on it until now.

"I'm going to ask the board to make me chairman emeritus and let me leave the organization. You will be chairman and chief executive officer. I recommend Elizabeth Commons as your president and chief operating officer, but that would only be with your approval. Here's the chart. You fill in the names and get it back to me by tomorrow morning.

"Hope you like this office. It'll be yours next week. Also, you'll have the honor of dealing with the press, the stock analysts, and the shareholders."

Harold was in shock. He just sat there staring. The chairman smiled at him.

"You'll get over it, you'll get over it. When I sent you off to talk to Ed Kargston, it was to see if you were just an overpaid accountant or someone who could be turned into an executive. Apparently, you've turned.

"You'll find there are no special skills involved in being an executive. It's a matter of deciding to do something and then dragging others along. Hopefully, you can do it in a way that will keep them smiling and enthusiastic, but one way or another it has to get done.

"We'll keep all this between ourselves until the meeting."

He stood up to shake hands and lead the still mute Harold to the outer office.

"You'll think about dividing this office into a couple of conference rooms for everyone else, with just a small place for you. Don't do anything with it for a year. You'll find it a very pleasant way to work, and it continually reminds people of where they are," Wallace said.

Harold walked back to his office, went inside, and closed the door. He dialed the phone.

"Ed?" he said. "You're not going to believe this, but you just graduated your first student. Would you like to take on a whole group of new ones?"

13
Alvin

Overcoming the
"Short-Term" Orientation

"Big corporation executive life is one thing," said Alvin, "but it isn't necessarily the real world. Most of the growth we see today comes from smaller companies. What's the big difference in leading between those two?"

Ed smiled and nodded.

"There are differences. The executives in the large corporation world are more concerned about themselves than the company. The company's success doesn't necessarily mean their personal success, and vice versa. Therefore, it's harder to get things done in a large organization just because everything has to go through a 'what-will-this-do-to-me?' evaluation.

"In smaller companies the executive relates more to the success of the organization. Things are more intimate. The effects of failure as well as success are felt very personally. Large companies, for instance, can have negative earnings for years before it all catches up to them. There is very little the individual executive can do to make those earnings higher or lower. Small companies have less room for problems. Wrong or lazy decisions can kill them quickly.

"MBA schools, where much executive thinking originates,

concentrate on making the individual successful, not on making companies successful. This makes sense for them because very few companies come to school; their customers are individuals. Management books usually are aimed at individuals. So in big companies executives think like individuals. In small companies they have a better chance of thinking like the company."

The Problem of Articulating the Problem

"Our purchasing organization is a small company," Alvin replied. "We spend a lot of money providing a service to the operations. They send us the request, we find the supplier, they receive the material, and they pay the bill. So I would like to think of myself as an executive in this type of company. We don't have divisions to buy or sell. We don't have any real assets. There are just a couple of hundred people buying stuff for other people to use.

"Our assets lie both in knowing the suppliers and in understanding the transaction process. We deal with finance, with quality, and with relationships."

"I think dealing with purchasing as a separate company in our talks could be very useful," said Ed. "It focuses on the executive clearly in terms of making the organization successful. You know, that's something that has just dawned on me recently. I've always been oriented toward making the organization work out somehow. It never occurred to me that others felt differently. Anyway, where shall we start? How about with old faithful: What's your biggest problem?"

Alvin smiled.

"My biggest problem is two problems really, but they're related. First, our customers don't specify clearly what they want; and, second, our suppliers don't deliver what they say they are going to deliver. The result of these two problems is a situation in which complete turmoil reigns. Every time my phone rings, it's someone with an emergency.

"'The shipment is late.' 'Inspection has rejected it.' 'The

supplier has not been paid for the last two orders.' 'That's an obsolete number.' 'We can't find it.' And it goes on like that all day."

Alvin was becoming emotional about all this. He didn't want to appear distressed to Ed, but it was becoming clear that he really didn't know how to get things under control.

"Sounds pretty normal to me," said Ed. "That's the way every purchasing department I ever saw worked. Traditionally, there is very little concern with anything except cost and delivery, all of which is short-range oriented."

"Well, it's time for a change," noted Alvin. "That's not being recognized throughout the profession yet, but it will be one day. However, it's not just a matter of our doing things better. A lot of people are involved. It's easy to say 'Think long-range,' but that can't happen unless it's possible to get a completely different input and direction from our customers. They have to tell us what they're going to want down the road," said Alvin.

"There are a lot of problems," said Ed. "Tell me, what's your vision of all this? What would the ideal purchasing department look like? How would it operate? What are the big differences? Who stands in the way of making all that happen?"

Alvin stared at him.

"The 'ideal purchasing department'? An interesting thought. Actually, we need to describe the ideal purchasing process. The department is just one component of it all."

Ed nodded in agreement.

"I'd recommend that you try to put your concepts into just a few, one-line statements that we can use to talk to people," he suggested. "It's okay to be a fanatic on something but only if that something can be explained quickly. The reason fanatics turn people off is because they ramble on and on. They're so obsessed with their subject and are so sure that no one else has even a basic understanding of it that they just erupt in total recall. They bury their victims in information and, as a result, turn them off, perhaps forever."

"All right, Ed," replied Alvin. "Let's assume that we can

put the whole situation into three or four statements, and let's assume that people understand them and even don't disagree too much with the ideas. What do we do then?"

"That's the executive part, Alvin," said Ed. "That's the one that makes something happen. We're not talking random philosophy here. We're after changing the way people do business. We're talking revolution and guerilla warfare. There is no profession that has escaped the opportunity to issue thick hides to those who believe in the conventional wisdom, and every function has them. They're hard to change."

Head to Head Against the Guardians of the Status Quo

Ed was getting involved in this project himself.

"The reason most revolutions fail," he continued, "is because those who are advancing on the castle think everyone else is right there with them. I would wager that not even all your own organization thinks this is a cause worth dying for. You may be the only one who is in a rage about it.

"After all, it's always been like this, hasn't it? Do you remember a time in your 18 or so years in the business that things have been different?"

Alvin shook his head.

"No, it has always been so," he said. "The mentors I had while I was learning the business were convinced that this is the way it is. They organized around it. They practically invented the purchasing holding crib, which is the place they stored things rejected by quality until the supplier could come fix them or engineering could be talked into accepting the nonconformances. I used to argue with them but the proof was all around us."

"So it will do no good to try refinement," said Ed. "We have to cut off the head of the old system and revitalize the entire situation. But you're in a position to do it. First, think out the new concept, and I suspect you've already done that. Then lay out the battle plan. Last, of course, is to enlist an army. What now? Where do we stand?"

Alvin stared at him for a moment.

"I do have some things I've been working on," he said. "Let me have a couple of days and I'll make you an offer you can't understand, as the Mafia lawyer is supposed to have said. At any rate, I will appreciate your evaluation of the approach and concepts. If it works, the organization will make dramatic strides, and I'll be a big hero. If it doesn't work, well, we'll cross that welfare line when we get there."

Ed agreed and rose to bid farewell. After Ed had left the office, Alvin turned to his computer and ran through the monthly acceptance figures posted by corporate quality. He had been studying them for several days searching for some pattern or hint that would set him on the right road. So far it had been futile.

The products and services were broken into categories and specific names in a standard fashion. So it was possible to look at customer results in comparative terms. Software was a persistent problem with all the recipients. There seemed to be no satisfactory way of testing it upon arrival, so it wasn't until someone began to apply it that problems were identified. At that moment, 32 software programs were undergoing rework or analysis. Since only 41 had ever been ordered, this indicated a significant problem.

Software for computer programs was the most difficult item the group dealt with. Although there were many standard packages around, people always wanted something special. The rejection rate was 100 percent because the satisfaction level was low. People continually changed their minds on software as they learned more about the jobs they were doing.

Machined products usually lead the list of defective material, and in this case it was fairly standard to see rejections of 15 percent. Alvin suspected that much of this rejection was due to the ease with which such products could be measured. Everyone liked to use inspection surface plates, and the new laser systems permitted exact measurement accompanied by printouts. The best part was that most of them were used anyway after material review.

Electronic assemblies were not a great deal of trouble, but individual components had quality levels that wavered all over. Some suppliers never had a rejection. Others were consistently nonconforming when delivering the same part.

Schedule was the other critical item. At any moment about 35 percent of all deliveries were behind schedule. It was very rare for something to arrive early, and attempts to begin a "just-in-time" inventory program had been unsuccessful except for off-the-shelf items.

We can get toilet paper and canned goods on short notice. Everything else is a big deal, Alvin mused to himself. Quality and schedule are both uncertain. Cost is not a great difficulty except when it comes to arguing about who pays for rework or unplanned changes. I need to get more information on that, he thought to himself.

The next day Alvin convened a meeting of two senior agents, two managers of purchasing, and two quality directors. They represented a cross section of his "small company." He arranged to serve them sandwiches and soft drinks in the conference room so they could get back to work on time. They were not pleased with being yanked away from the battlefield.

"I'm glad all of you were able to join me for lunch, such as it is," said Alvin. "I just wanted to chat a little bit about our mission. Someone challenged me the other day to describe an 'ideal purchasing operation.' I wanted to get your ideas, without a lot of preplanning, as to what the world would look like if we could do it our way. And, of course, I need to know what 'our way' is."

He paused and looked around. There was complete silence.

"My review of our results shows that we do well on handling cost, but quality and schedule are completely variable. One day we're great; the next we're a disaster. If we could put the great days together, we would do well. But the pattern I see puts us in the disaster court more often lately. What do you think?"

AGENT ONE: The biggest problem we would have in creating the ideal system is changing the ways of our customer. We never get clear requirements, except in standard products; and then we're never allowed enough time.

AGENT TWO: I agree that the customer is the problem. The groups I work with refuse to do anything in writing. They want to place all orders on the phone; and if I don't watch them, they call the suppliers directly. By the time it comes from them, through me, and on to the supplier, we're lucky to get anything that's even close to what they want.

MANAGER ONE: The suppliers are my biggest problem. They all want to be sole source. They don't like to bid on anything. We try to get them to select some senior official to deal with us, but it always reverts to the minor leagues. The senior people are too busy going to our top management to spend time bidding on orders.

MANAGER TWO: We need more latitude in selecting suppliers. The quality people need to give us a list of those companies we can depend on to do good work. We have no way of knowing which are going to perform. Also, we need to get more consistent in the receiving areas. Some days everything is rejected, and some days it all goes through.

QUALITY ONE: All we do is check the incoming shipment to the purchase order, and it either meets it or it doesn't. We don't reject or accept goods according to the way we feel, and I resent the implication.

QUALITY TWO: And as for picking suppliers who are going to perform, well, we've tried that. In fact, we provide you all with a list of several hundred we feel are acceptable, and we keep it up-to-date. The list is based on the results of our receiving work and on audits we do to companies who apply for listing. The problem is purchasing only buys to the lowest price.

MANAGER TWO: That's not exactly true, but we do get criticized when we fail to pick the low price. We have to show that the selected firm does something better or that quality doesn't like the low-bid outfit.

AGENT ONE: I've been a purchasing agent for almost 40 years now, and I've had this same meeting at least every two years. It's going to get nowhere, Alvin. None of us know the answer. If we did, we would have told you about it.

QUALITY TWO: We need to get tougher with the suppliers. You all treat them with kid gloves. Any time we complain about one of them, your guys are all over us to get more reasonable.

AGENT TWO: We have to keep the goods flowing. If we listened to quality, we would have empty bins.

MANAGER ONE: Sometimes I think that empty bins would be better than the mixed bag we have now.

ALVIN: Our inventory is contaminated?

MANAGER ONE: Some of it's old. Some of it has limited use due to waivers. Some of it's okay. Some of it's out of date. I would say, without having the facts to back it up, that 25 percent of our inventory is not useful.

ALVIN: That's a lot of money, and it doesn't speak well for our organization. Is there any way we can get a factual evaluation?

QUALITY TWO: The internal auditors have been working with us on sampling the inventory. The results will be available soon, but the betting is that 25 percent might be a low number.

ALVIN: We don't seem to have a unified policy on all this.

AGENT ONE: It's impossible because our customers refuse to cooperate.

MANAGER TWO: This is not a field in which cooperation is something that leaps immediately to mind. It's always been chaotic because there is no long-range plan. Nobody knows what we'll be buying next month. There are a lot of standard and usual items, of course, but most of it is routinely different. We're a big-job shop.

ALVIN: I want to thank all of you for coming by. I'll keep you informed on whatever is going to happen. I really appreciate your leveling with me about what's going on. Thanks.

The participants departed, leaving Alvin to sit in the conference room by himself. When his administrative assistant finally found him, he had come to the conclusion that this organization was definitely not going to heal itself. Someone would have to devise a prescription that would bring this mess to some sort of order. It was apparent to him that the participants were stuck in the mud and couldn't see the grass, let alone the trees or any light at the end of the tunnel. They were helpless. Well, as Ed would say: This is where executives earn their perks.

TO: Purchasing Management
FROM: Alvin Austin
SUBJECT: Department strategy

The traditional problems of purchasing have long been known to us. They consist primarily of inadequately stated customer requirements, informational errors generated by us, and incomplete performance by the suppliers.

Efforts have been made over the years, both formally and informally, to put all of this into an orderly and efficient system. Those efforts have had varying success. However, we are able to carry out our mission primarily because we have dedicated and sincere people and because there is a lot of experience among us. We need to provide a system that does not need so much artificial support. Our customers share very little common culture and consist of many scattered operations working on many different things. That places us in the position of being a small company trying to deal with a wide variety of customers and suppliers. We have to look at it as though we were independent because if we do not perform, our customers have the right to do their own buying. They would prefer, I am sure, not to have the overhead expense of paying for our services, and they would avoid that transaction if they bought for themselves. So it is important that we serve them promptly and efficiently.

In order to place our situation in concrete terms, our financial operations have performed at my request an analysis to see how efficient we are. They took our job descriptions, our purpose-of-travel reports, the purchase order change notices, and their own observations to come up with the following. This information is obviously incomplete but will be firmer as we gain experience.

"DO-IT-OVER" BREAKDOWN

Trips made to correct problems, in percent	57%
Purchases for which changes were issued	43%
Customers complaining on a daily basis	76%
Received orders rejected by customer quality	19%
Orders received late by customers	27%
Suppliers who call for more information	38%

A look at these percentages shows that we spend a lot of time walking back over trails we have already traveled. We have to learn how to do things much better. I think we essentially need to begin again with a whole new way of operating. I am going to provide some basic direction on our concepts and the system for implementation. After you have absorbed that, I am going to ask you to a special meeting where we will work on details and assign the tasks for accomplishment. Some of what we are going to do will involve capital expenses, but headquarters is agreeable to funding that. Here are the basics:

1. We will cease being the purchasing department and be-come acquisition operations. This will let us take a broader approach with our customers and suppliers.

2. We will install computer terminals in customer offices and in the offices of our larger suppliers. This will let the cus-tomer prepare the acquisition description in tandem with us. Through data cooperation, the originator and the ac-quiring agent will be able to agree on the purchase de-scription before it ever hits a piece of paper. Then it can be transferred immediately to the supplier without wast-ing time on mail. Everyone will have immediate under-standing.

3. We will set up classroom education for customers, our-selves, and suppliers. We will have courses on acquisition management, on being a supplier to our company, how to describe what needs to be supplied, and several other ar-eas. No customer, supplier, or employee will escape the net.

4. We will issue a clear policy that says we expect everyone to be committed to on-time delivery of conforming products or services at the agreed price. We will eliminate all op-portunities to deviate from that.

5. We will begin to measure the expense of inefficiency on a regular basis and include it in our financial reports.

6. A friend told me that we needed to get our business down to three sentences that we could repeat on command when the situation required it. I think these are the sen-tences:

   • Our job is to take the acquisition-management actions that provide our customers with material and services that exactly fill their determined needs.

   • Our job is to carefully identify and select suppliers who consistently provide what we need and help in the de-termination of that need.

- Our job is to help everyone involved through continual professional innovation.

Change Management

"How's it all turning out?" asked Ed.

"Well, the customers and the suppliers like the idea of being tied directly to us by computer. We have it now to the point that all three parties can agree on something within a day. That's taken a lot of pressure off the scheduling aspect of the business and has nearly eliminated the need for purchase order changes. We're arranging for suppliers to invoice us by wire and for us to pay them by wire. With any luck we could stop mailing paper around soon."

"And how's the school going?" asked Ed.

"That's what I thought would be the easiest part," said Alvin. "I figured we would just bring people here, stand up in front of them, explain it all, and everything would start to work beautifully. What I learned was that education is a difficult task. It takes a great deal of preparation, and we would've had to spend some money on films and workbooks, which we didn't know how to do anyway.

"I hired a consulting firm to do it all for us. They've set us up with what they call a 'client-taught' class. Many of the things I thought *I* invented, it turns out, were ideas and concepts they've been using for some time. But it all worked out, and it's been inexpensive this way."

"How about software? Is that solvable?" asked Ed.

"We're getting better at it. We insist that the customer spend more time describing exactly what the program is supposed to do. Then the supplier works that out in the proper terms and sits down with the customer until both agree. Then they make a pact not to do any changing. That's lengthened the time it takes to write the specification, but it has cut the programming time greatly and has eliminated checkout or 'debugging' time. The satisfaction rate is much higher now."

"So your problems are all gone?" said Ed.

"Hardly," smiled Alvin. "Much to my surprise, our people haven't been all that cooperative. All these changes have bothered them, I suspect."

"People tend to see changes as job threatening. Improvement scares them because they only see that some work doesn't have to be done anymore," stated Ed.

"I guess I know that," said Alvin. "But I never really believed it until now. That means we didn't do a complete job on this transformation. We didn't let the employees have any personal participation in putting this change process together. I assumed they would be happy."

"Don't assume that they're unhappy," said Ed. "Happy or unhappy are all relative things. But you can assume that they're uninformed. Your letter said that all employees would have to be informed. Have they been?"

Alvin shook his head sadly.

"Not much. We've been working so hard on bringing all the professionals together that we haven't done much orientation. The consultants wanted to do a program on that, but the feeling was that we could wait. I think that might have been a foolish decision," mumbled Alvin.

"Well, it isn't too late to do something about it," said Ed. "I would suggest that an orientation program be put together soon and that a committee of people representing all areas and several levels of responsibility be formed to talk about it first. Let the consultants interview them. Then the program that results will be something the folks will identify with."

"Good idea," said Alvin. "We'll do it like that, and I promise never to forget that in the future."

"Oh, you'll forget it," smiled Ed. "But when someone or some incident reminds you, there'll be no doubt about the corrective action to take."

14

Graduation Celebration

The group gathered at Ed's home for their graduation lunch. He had decided that this would give them the opportunity to be more relaxed. The process had been operating for most of a year now, and his next class had conducted their first general discussion meeting. Ed Kargston Associates wasn't just Ed Kargston anymore. It actually had a few associates now. Ed would have a dual-education job over the next year.

"This was a wonderful idea," said Elizabeth. "I'm delighted that you made an executive decision and invited all of us to come visit you. How long have you lived here?"

Ed cocked his head.

"Sixteen years, I think," he said. "We came out here when I became president of Estate. My first executive decision after that was that I would never miss a weekend here."

"How'd that one turn out?" asked Alvin.

"It wasn't always easy," said Ed, "but I held to it. And I never missed dinner at home if I was in town. The kids have commented on that many times, particularly now that they're in business."

"Do you attribute that to personal discipline?" asked Elizabeth.

"No, personal policy. That's what lets people go ahead and do what they should do—policy," replied Ed.

As the group gathered and exchanged small talk, Ed noticed that they were completely comfortable with each other. There was no competitive spirit. There were no concerns about what the others might be hiding or planning.

"Okay, team," he said, "now that we're all through with the welcomes and catch-ups, we need to get to work. What I would like to do to see if you've earned your sheepskins is to ask each of you to talk a little about what you've learned, if anything, during the time we've been working together.

"I suspect the list will be fairly short because you would've been learning anyway, and what we've been doing has been a special experience. Let's begin with the new president of Eastland. Elizabeth?"

"Well, as I said into your tape recorder, I finally understand the difference between an executive and a manager. I quit reacting and started acting. Now that I have reached the level I've always complained about, it's good to be able to reach out and do things. Fortunately, my boss went to the same school, so he doesn't spend much time second-guessing me."

She smiled at Harold, who clenched his hands over his head.

"She wouldn't pay too much attention anyway, but we're working well together," said Harold.

"While you're talking, what did you learn?" asked Ed.

"I learned from the course a lot about what an executive does. I've become a much more decisive person who's not quite so concerned with not rocking boats.

"But I think the best lesson I received was from Wallace Smith. Once he finally found his successor, he just packed up his office and went home. We send him mail and such, and most of it just disappears into a pit somewhere. He's doing all kinds of things, and none of them have anything to do with the company. He still comes to the board meetings but just sits there and smiles most of the day."

Nick set down his glass and looked at Harold.

"What's the lesson from Mr. Smith?"

"The lesson, my son," said Harold, with mock arrogance, "is that once you've made a decision of that magnitude, you carry it out. Just walk off and don't worry about it. He waited all that time for someone to come in and take charge. I didn't even realize I was doing it. All I wanted to do was change our culture. He wanted to change it, too, but seemed to have run out of gas in that area."

"As we age," said Ed, "we sometimes can see the struggles things could cause and tend to back away from them. There're a lot of useful things to do without mounting a crusade every year."

"I know it isn't my turn yet," said Nick, "but the most powerful lesson I learned was that changing something is hard work. Thinking up the concepts, explaining them so that people can understand, and then laying out the plan for implementation are difficult. However, that's the easy part. Getting people to *do* things differently, to *work* at putting the change into effect is just plain hard—exciting and rewarding, but hard."

"I learned that it's easy to dive into detail work in order to avoid what you're talking about, Nick," said Alvin. "I'm noticing that oftentimes executives are busy, busy, busy, so they won't have to do any real work. They have all this stuff going on and tend to work long hours, yet very little actually gets done that wouldn't get done anyway.

"I realize that this is heresy, but I'm beginning to believe that if they all quit coming to work, it wouldn't make much difference."

Anna giggled.

"Don't say that around our bank. We all take ourselves very seriously. What I've learned is that it's possible to get so wrapped up in the product or the system that we forget all about people. We bankers tend to think that if the numbers add up, everything must be in good shape.

"And I agree with Nick. To use a cliché, 'it's like pulling teeth.' But there's more to it than that. It's pulling them out, cleaning everything up, and then replacing each tooth exactly as before—all on a dead run."

"At any rate, I'm enjoying myself much more," said Harold. "I realize that I used to worry so much about the other executives and the boss and what was going to be criticized that I wasn't working. I wouldn't let policies be laid out because I was afraid someone would object."

As they chatted, Ed watched proudly and decided that this was going to be a good venture. No one would realize how easy his job was. All he had to do was select bright, energetic people with solid integrity as a base. Then by removing them from the herd for awhile, they could be made to realize where their potential lay.

The characteristics of leadership could be explained to folks like that.

15

Guidelines for Browsers

Executives determine what is going to be run; managers do the running.   1

Without executives the managers would have nothing to manage.   1

Most of it [being an executive] is conceptual; a lot is energy; the majority is direction.   1

The ability to get the impossible done in a manager's job just means that even more impossible tasks will soon be on the way.   3

It never dawns on them [many senior executives] that the pieces on the chessboard are fixing the game in favor of those who appreciate them.   4

It is not possible to fool the people for very long. Once in a while they are wrong in judging those who are put over them, but they catch on very quickly.   4

If anything is certain, it is that change is certain. The world we are planning for today will not exist tomorrow in this form.   8

The business desert is layered with the bones of those who felt they understood completely and stopped learning.   8

In almost every business failure the situation as it developed was known and could have been prevented, just like most political disasters.   9

Making a wrong decision can be understood. Refusing to search continually for learning cannot be.   9

The best reputation a leader can possess relates to displaying ethical conduct in all things.   9

Those who cry for a list of what is and what is not ethical are going to always have problems along this line.   9

People want their leaders to be real people. They want to know that there is not a surrounding layer of underlings who prevent persons from reaching the executive with important information.   9

Subordinates establish their personal determination level based on what they see in their leader. Wimpy behavior produces wimpy results.   10

Enthusiasm is the result of an energetic person working on something that he or she finds keenly interesting. This means a leader should not accept any project that does not produce a tingle deep down.   10

Nothing makes an organization ineffective as quickly as the necessity to wonder about what is going to please or displease the boss.   10

Some who become executives feel that the power given to them grants permission to quit dealing with reality.   11

It is very easy for executives to come to the conclusion that they are the beginning and end of everything that is happening.   11

Few battles are lost because of a lack of courage or dedication on the part of the troops. The leadership has to set about almost deliberately to overcome the positive characteristics of their personnel if the operation is to fail.   14

Everything necessary for personal and corporate success lies within these three equal areas. They provide the foundation that carries and controls the organization.   15

Running a corporation is too important to be left up to the functional departments.   15

Policies have to cover all the bases and relate to all operations. They have to incorporate thinking that is worldwide, industrywide, and peoplewide.   16

Most companies...are working harder and smarter but have not taken the aggressive and positive steps that result in a permanent culture change.   19

If executives pass their creative responsibilities downward, then what happens will be based on local needs rather than corporate objectives.   22

Policy is not some archaic bit of brown paper hidden in leather-covered books positioned on everyone's credenza. Policy is what the organization does all the time. If none is established formally, then one will come forth on its own based on the previous experience of those involved.   22

Prevention must become the order of the day.   23

Relationships are where it all comes together or comes apart. Nothing else can be made to happen if relationships do not exist.   23

Unless someone states emphatically just what the "right things" are and are not, then others will use their judgments, which are inevitably based on a different agenda.   24

If the policies that cause a turnaround and make something happen are not continually reinforced and upgraded, the culture that created the original situation will regenerate.   25

The ecology of an organization is as delicate and vulnerable as that of a forest.   27

The tone of organizational relationships is established by executives, directly or indirectly. Insensitive management can eliminate a forest just as proper direction can help it become glorious.   27

Organizations glow or dim depending on how people perceive each other, how they work together, and how their actions interrelate.   27

Situations cannot be neglected on the premise that they will work themselves out; they usually will not.   28

We often do not realize how many people we need to work with in order to run our lives.   31

Companies have personalities but management teams do not. Each member sees the group differently, and although they act in a common cause, they usually do it for different reasons.   32

Some "purposeful conflict" is necessary for success, I suspect, but it can waste a lot of time if the purposefulness is not properly contained.   33

When requirements exist, it is possible to determine what the relationship is all about and get everything on a practical basis.   33

Almost everything that does not work got that way because of a relationship problem somewhere in its cycle. And hardly anything works.   34

Wars very rarely happen between people with a common understanding of goals and purposes.   35

No company is an island, as the poet came close to saying. Companies would have a difficult time surviving without suppliers, customers, participating employees, or financial sources.   35

Not all relationships are formally generated.   37

How many people do we know personally who know what they are doing? It is up to the executive to find them and make certain that they can exist happily in the organization.   38

No organization or forest can grow and prosper based on a series of one-night stands. People need to know where they stand and what is going on under the ground.   38

Every action taken by every employee involves quality. Most of the conversations held at the executive level concern things that have gone wrong, seem to be going wrong, or might go wrong.   39

Quality is the result of a carefully constructed culture environment. It has to be the fabric of the organization, not part of the fabric, but the actual fabric.   40

Not everyone is for quality. Sometimes it can seem like a good idea to have everything in turmoil in order to provide the opportunity of becoming famous by constructing a turnaround.   40

There is a great deal of evidence showing that change can be accomplished without spending much money or inflicting a great deal of pain. The solution comes down to a few understandings.   40

Quality means "conformance to requirements"; management's prime responsibility is to cause the right requirements to be created.   40

All action must be oriented around prevention.   41

Managers who learn to think in a preventive manner should be rewarded and recognized.   41

The policy of the company has to be that every individual will understand the requirements of his or her job and will conform to them.   41

When quality is defined as conformance to requirements, "goodness" has nothing to do with it.   41

Lack of compliance to these concepts and policies must be measured in financial terms as well as in customer satisfaction.   42

They have their troubles, but that is not where all the costs and waste lie. Most of it comes from the administrative and support areas.   46

As the executive establishes the ecology of the organization, prevention has to become an actual, integral part of policy.   52

The financial world, both professional and personal, is a forest of actual and potential "black holes" with magnetic strength sufficient to easily overcome an individual or a business.   53

In business you must understand any deal completely before becoming involved. There is not always someone there to bail you out.   55

Patience and discretion are the keys to not being trapped in a "black hole." It also helps to know exactly where all the money is coming from and where it is going.   57

Fortune 500 companies have several more zeros at the end of their numbers, but reporting and communicating requirements are very much the same.   60

It is not necessary to have a new office with dozens of people in order to experience unplanned costs. A tiny place with two people can make that happen, particularly if it is international.   60

People are revenue oriented and will always operate right at or beyond the amount of funds they see to be available in their crystal ball. They always think more will be forthcoming.   62

Expenses are the key to profitability. There is no revenue stream that cannot be outspent.   62

It is hard to find a company that failed because its expenses were too low. Those who erased themselves through not using resources properly are legion.   63

Just keeping neat records of overspending is not money management.   64

Financial integrity in an organization requires attention on a similar scale. Examination must be unrelenting, because success, like liberty, requires eternal vigilance.   66

It is not necessary to be noisy to be effective.   69

Most of being an executive comes down to attitude and smarts.   77

There's a lot more involved than just knowledge and intensity. Aspiring executives have to learn how to create the right work environment and do it on purpose.   78

Aspiring executives need a constancy of purpose if they are going to do something that lasts. If they are involved only in survival, for instance, nothing they do will be around for very long.   87

A lot of people condemn themselves to predetermined lifestyles through the attitudes they select. This is true in every area, not just with the executives we are trying to raise.   97

The oblivious executive is so concentrated on a private agenda that others do not enter into the equation at all. This is the "Mr. McGoo" style of management in which the "hero" bumbles along with no real idea of what is happening, yet somehow, miraculously, things fall into place.   98

The most significant problem in executive life is ego—ego both ways: too much and not enough.   99

If we could put together the leader's job description, it would be something like this:

1. Create the right environment—on purpose.
2. Reduce complex issues to something each person can understand and learn to handle.
3. Concentrate on the objectives of the operation.
4. Relate to people at all times.   101

Everything is personal. People don't want to separate home life and work life into categories. You say it; they register it.   102

If you have a make-believe world in the office, you get make-believe reactions.   102

When direction is conceived with one thought in mind and implemented with quite another, then it becomes clear just how complex the business of being an executive really is.   112

Leaders have to be smarter than the average bear. They have to be able to comprehend situations quickly, take on a large load of data without much trouble, think longer-term than others, and be able to translate thought into action.   112

When people stop thinking, it means that the executive has somehow flipped their switch. To put it another way, if they think you're going to think of it, they don't have to think of it; so they don't.   116

It's quite possible to have a negative effect while trying very hard to do things just the opposite.   127

Arrogance is one of the primary causes of executive failure, and plain old egotism is right behind it. However, arrogance is curable while egotism may not be.   127

Sometimes we can overmanage things. The key is to avoid having to manage yourselves, just to be natural.   129

Whenever the person with the most power steps into a picture, everyone else pulls back.   131

An organization is a body, and every part has to be nourished.   138

If you're halfway smart and appear confident, you can get almost anything done in the depths of a big organization. They think you know what you're doing.   145

Don't go around asking permission to do what you already are commissioned to do. But don't stomp on someone just because they happen to be in the way.   146

Eliminating what is not wanted or needed is profitable in itself.　149

Successful people breed success.　149

The only way to grow continually is to be a real part of every economy. Then you can have customers everywhere.　149

The key to a useful and satisfying life, at least the part we human beings can do something about, lies in the willingness to learn and continue learning.　150

To lead, you have to be concentrated, or focused, on something that you want to happen. And the leader has to get the message across to those who will carry it out.　154

The process of arriving at consensus can develop peace and quiet, but it rarely produces innovation and excitement. Such things usually originate with an individual.　155

Consensus should be used for implementation but not for determination.　155

It is not the doing that creates division, it is the conceiving of what to do.　155

The working environment is everything. The culture is part of it. A culture can be overcome and drowned by a negative environment.　179

It's harder to get things done in a large organization just because everything has to go through a "what-will-this-do-for-me?" evaluation.　185

In smaller companies the executive relates more to the success of the organization. Things are more intimate. The effects of failure as well as success are felt very personally.　185

MBA schools, where much executive thinking originates, concentrate on making the individual successful, not on making companies successful.　185

It's okay to be a fanatic on something but only if that something can be explained quickly.　187

Index

Ability, 3, 203, 210
Acceptance, 37–38
Accounting, 28, 49, 57, 58
Accounts payable, 61
Accounts receivable, 50, 51, 61
Ad hoc policy, 116–119
Advertising, 2, 20
Army Ballistic Missile Agency
    (ABMA), 28–30
Arrogance, 127–128, 210
Articulation, 186–188
Assertiveness, 38
Attention, 154–160
Attitude, 12, 49, 77, 97–99, 209
Automobile industry, 18
Availability, 7, 9–10, 204

Benefits, 63
Budget, 61–62, 140, 141
Business distress, 8
Business failure, 9, 204
Busyness, 201, 212

Cash flow, 22, 24, 50, 51, 57, 59, 62
Cash retention, 43
Catalytic action, 28, 30
Change, 8–9, 40, 50–51, 145–149,
    196–197, 203–205, 207, 212

Churchill, Winston, 14, 88–89, 92
Client awareness, 134
Commitment, 41–42
Communications, 8, 29–30, 33–34,
    145–149
Compensation, 63
Compliance, 42, 207
Comprehension, 112, 210
Concentration, 113, 154, 211
Confidence, 2, 10, 17, 145, 210
Conflict, 33, 206
Conformance, 40–41
Consensus, 154–155, 211
Constancy of purpose, 87, 209
Consulting visits, 32
Corporate culture, 19–21, 39–40,
    179, 181–183, 211
Corporate overhaul, 171–183
Corporate policy, 16, 22–25, 50,
    116–119, 205
Corporate strategy, 137–151
Courage, 14, 204
Creative responsibility, 22, 78, 87,
    205, 209
Culture, corporate, 19–21, 39–40,
    179, 181–183, 211
Culture change, 19, 205
Culture shock, 17

Customer satisfaction, 24, 207

Debt, 63
Debt servicing, 57
Decision making, 9, 204
Dedication, 14, 204
Defect-free, 41
Deliberateness, 38
Determination, 8, 10
Direction, 1, 24, 112, 203, 210
Discretion, 57, 208
Dividends, 63

Ecology, 27, 52, 205, 208
Effectiveness, 10, 69, 204, 209
Egotism, 99, 128, 209
80-20 rule, 144
Eisenhower, Dwight, 14–15, 88, 92
Empathy, 28
Employee input, 50–51
Employee turnover, 51, 176, 179
Energy, 1, 8, 10, 15, 203
Engineering, 16, 20, 28
Enthusiasm, 10, 204
Ethics, 7, 9, 204
Executives, 1–2, 8–15, 22, 69–70, 154, 178, 185, 200, 203, 211, 212
Expenses, 63–64, 208

Finance, 2, 15, 16, 20, 23–25, 50, 53–66, 86, 87, 105–108, 166, 208, 209
Financial reporting, 63–64
Foreign competition, 17–19
Fortune 500 companies, 16, 60, 208
Functional specialists, 15–16, 18

Generally accepted operating customs (GAOC), 21
Gross profit, 64

Head-in-the-sand school of management, 109–113

Humbleness, 8, 11–12

Information flow, 8
Innovation, 113–116
Intensity, 8, 12
Interpersonal skills, 2

Jesus of Nazareth, 89
Job description, 101–102, 209
Just-in-time delivery system, 49

Labor rates, 18
Leadership, 2–3, 7–13, 154, 211
Learn, willingness to, 7–9, 149–151
Lincoln, Abraham, 88, 92
Line of credit, 64–65

Malaise, 48–50, 55–57
Management teams, 32, 33, 206
Managers, 1–2, 22, 41, 178, 200, 203, 207
Manufacturing companies, 42
Margin, 43
Marketing, 16, 20–21
Market share, 18, 21
Marshall, George, 92
Mass production, 17
MBAs, 85–86, 175–176, 185–186, 211
Mentors, 188
Money management, 64, 208
Mr. McGoo management style, 98, 209

Napoleon, 14, 88
Net profit, 65
Noncompliance, 42
Nonconformance, 48

Opportunities, 2
Organizational relationships, 27–28
Organizations, 14, 27, 128, 178, 206, 207, 210
Orientation, 185–196
Overmanagement, 129, 210

Patience, 57, 208
Performance appraisals, 24, 177
Permission, getting, 146, 210
Personal agendas and goals, 40
Personality, 32, 206
Personnel, 20
Planning, 130
Pleasantness, 8, 13
Power, 11–12, 131, 204, 210
Prevention, 23, 41, 51–52, 138,
    205, 207
Priorities, reevaluation of, 142–145
Proaction, 15–19
Problem identification, 17
Productivity, 179
Profit, 43, 62, 149, 208
Proposal Action Requests (PARs),
    173, 181
Public relations, 179–180
Purchasing, 16, 20, 49, 186–188

Quality, 8, 15, 16, 18, 19, 23, 25,
    28, 39–52, 86, 87, 119–121,
    166, 207
Quality management, 47, 48

Reaction, 15–19
Recognition programs, 51
Relationships, 2, 15, 23, 25, 27–38,
    69, 86, 87, 123–136, 166, 205,
    206
Reliability, 8, 10–11
Reputation, 9, 204
Research and development, 20

Resolve, 78–79
Retained cash, 43
Revenues, 65
Roosevelt, Franklin D., 15, 92

Sales, 65
Satisfaction, personal, 1
Sensibility, 8, 11
Sensitivity, 153–169
Service companies, 42
Smartness, 77, 112–113, 145, 210
Stalin, Joseph, 88
Statistical-process control charts,
    119–120
Status quo, 188–196
Staywithitness, 130–132
Steel industry, 18
Subordinates, 10, 204
Success, 4, 14–15, 33, 149, 185,
    205, 209, 211
Survival, 206, 209

Television industry, 18
Textile industry, 18
Thinking, 116, 130, 210
Truman, Harry, 132

Unions, 18

Von Braun, Wernher, 28

Wilson, Woodrow, 131–132
Wonder Woman syndrome,
    115–116

About the Author

Phil Crosby is well-known as the prime mover in the "quality revolution." He has been for 36 years. Formerly vice president at ITT and now chairman of Philip Crosby Associates, Inc., he is one of our most highly respected and sought after international management consultants and educators. Crosby is among the best-selling authors in the field, with such outstanding quality and management works to his credit as *Quality is Free*, *Quality Without Tears*, *Running Things*, *The Eternally Successful Organization*, and *Let's Talk Quality*.